# The Horror Show

# Vincenzo Bilof

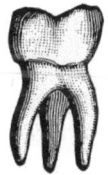

**Bizarro Pulp Press**
an imprint of JournalStone Publishing

Copyright © 2013 by Vincenzo Bilof

All rights reserved. No part of this book may be used or reproduced by any means, graphic, electronic, or mechanical, including photocopying, recording, taping or by any information storage retrieval system without the written permission of the publisher except in the case of brief quotations embodied in critical articles and reviews.

This is a work of fiction. All of the characters, names, incidents, organizations, and dialogue in this novel are either the products of the author's imagination or are used fictitiously.

Bizarro Pulp Press books may be ordered through booksellers or by contacting:

Bizarro Pulp Press, a JournalStone imprint
www.BizarroPulpPress.com

The views expressed in this work are solely those of the authors and do not necessarily reflect the views of the publisher, and the publisher hereby disclaims any responsibility for them.

ISBN: 978-0-615874-84-5

Printed in the United States of America
JournalStone rev. date: May 7, 2015

Cover Art: P.A. Douglas
Interior Art: William Cook
Interior Formatting by: Lori Michelle
www.theauthorsalley.com

# Contents

Forewarned ..................................................................................i

## CHAPTER ONE The Distance Between Two Worlds
7:00 AM Windows ......................................................................3
Motorcyclical.............................................................................5
Eye Stains .................................................................................7
Pretty Girls ................................................................................9
Casual Ruinations ...................................................................10
An Intimate Confessional .......................................................12
When She Needs Herself .......................................................14
Caged-Tunnel Lucidity ...........................................................15
Time Unknown .......................................................................18
An Honest Review..................................................................21
Echoes of a Child's Mirage ....................................................22
Awake ....................................................................................24
Other Women ........................................................................25
We Boldly Go to Nowhere .....................................................28

## CHAPTER TWO (YEARS AGO) Affairs in Order
Catholic Homicide...................................................................31
Sepia Tonal .............................................................................34
Dirt Roads, Snake Pits ...........................................................35
We Can Be Metaphors ...........................................................37
Nous Faisons Tout pour l'Amour ...........................................39

## CHAPTER THREE (Lorraine) The Grand Experiment
Reactionaries .........................................................................45
The Questions a Madwoman Might Ask ...............................47
This Feeling for You ...............................................................49
Hanged by a Thread ..............................................................51
The Invisible Treatise .............................................................52
Law Giver ...............................................................................53
Love Song Written for the Amnesiac ....................................55
Love Song Written for the Narcoleptic ..................................57
Love Song Written for the Poet .............................................58

## CHAPTER FOUR (The Doctor) Hippocrates Weeps
- Words of Advice ..... 63
- Common Diagnosis ..... 64
- Free Money ..... 66
- Second Opinion ..... 67
- The Disconsolate Opinion ..... 69
- Searching for Shelly ..... 70
- Paid For ..... 73
- The Science of Strangulation ..... 76

## CHAPTER FIVE (The Poet) Words That Spell Rage
- Bile, Remembrances, Shards ..... 81
- Past Tense ..... 86
- Precipitate Palms ..... 88
- Loading the Years ..... 94

## CHAPTER SIX Visitation with the Ghosts
- Intestinal ..... 97
- Cutter ..... 98
- Remembering that Day ..... 100
- Love's Tattered Phase ..... 102
- Watching the Sun Burn ..... 105

## CHAPTER SEVEN Interview with the Witnesses, Character and Otherwise
- Evening News ..... 113
- Look at this Poem ..... 115
- Suffering with Strangers (Excerpt from Interview, 2003) ..... 118
- Lover at the End of Time ..... 120
- The Starch Monsters ..... 122
- Street Testament ..... 125
- Razor Blurred ..... 127
- Lorraine ..... 129
- He Took Me to a Ballgame ..... 132
- CONNIE ..... 133
- Parks in Reverse ..... 136
- Fractional Semi-Fiction ..... 137

## CHAPTER EIGHT (Fragments, Evidence) Echoes from the American Crypt
- Foreword ..... 143

Colonies on Fire ................................................................144
A Collection of Weddings ...............................................145
Biography of a Lucid Dream............................................146
Rainbows Jade the Chamber ...........................................147
Hands Cut from Plastic....................................................148
Horses While Chained ....................................................149
The Killer's Catharsis.......................................................151
Angel Holocaust ..............................................................156

**CHAPTER NINE (The Poet) Puppet without Limbs**
The Late Show.................................................................163
The Poet's Deliberate Dream: Part 1................................166
The Poet's Deliberate Dream: The Sequel ......................167
Boiled Scream .................................................................168
Murder Mongrel ..............................................................171
The Poet's Deliberate Dream Part Three: Untitled .........173
Jester Pyre .......................................................................174
Junkyard Plain ................................................................175
Verona, Where We Lay ...................................................177

**CHAPTER TEN(The Poet and the Victim) Asleep at a Funeral**
Memento of Truth ...........................................................181
Moments of You ..............................................................182
Words on a Bridge ..........................................................184
Sonnet X ..........................................................................186
Sequels Collide ...............................................................188

**CHAPTER ELEVEN (The Poet) Afterbirth**
Allusion to a Brief Candle ..............................................193
Speaking through the Moon ..........................................194
The Gods and their Action Figure..................................195
Pretty Pictures ................................................................197
(Words Left on Her Pillow) ............................................198
Colorful Birds .................................................................200
No More Monkeys ..........................................................202
Nerve Endings ................................................................204

**CHAPTER TWELVE Visitations Again**
Love Song for the Prisoner.............................................209
We Can Feel Sad Now ....................................................212
Mrs Every ........................................................................213

If Only We Could Die Again ........................................................... 215
Operant Conditioning .................................................................. 217

## CHAPTER THIRTEEN Upon an Ivory Coast
The Students (When I Can See Again) ........................................... 221
Erasure ......................................................................................... 222
Like a Scene from a Movie that Might Not Be Good Anymore .... 229
If Ulysses Wore His Sunglasses ..................................................... 230
The Sex of the Ocean .................................................................... 231
IN THE NAME OF SCIENCE ......................................................... 234
Dear Danny, .................................................................................. 239

## EPILOGUE: (Voices Underwater) Puzzle Pieces
"Let's See What's on the Two O'Clock News" .............................. 243
"It's Already Quarter to Three?" ................................................... 245
The Return of the Prisoner ........................................................... 247
Sale for the Century ..................................................................... 248
The Sound of an Epilogue in an Empty Theater .......................... 251
Confessions from the Street Generation, In the Year 2001 in the Month
   of April ..................................................................................... 253

# Forewarned

You know the saying: Forewarned is forearmed. I wonder if it could also be "four-footed". I wonder a lot of things.
    Knock knock.
    Who's there?
    The doorbell. Why does everybody keep knocking?!!
    Sorry, that just popped into my head. I really meant to say that I have been asked to introduce this book of, well, very unusual poems by the guy whose name is on the cover. We can pause a moment for you to go back and check, in case you've forgotten.
    La dee dah, hmmm-hmmm-hmmm, dum-dee-dum . . .
    Oh, you know who wrote it? You're just not sure about me? I see. Join the club! Get in line! There are plenty of people like that running around, believe me. Nonetheless, here we are and here I am too. Although I am not really all here. At least, that's what the people say before they start running. But let's not get into that. It probably had something to do with a chainsaw accident at birth. Ever since then, there is a part of me that follows behind my steps, leaving a trail of slobber, tending to get lost, taking wrong turns and wandering off cliffs. Please ignore it. I do. It's one of those eye-rolling issues in life that you simply have to accept and move on . . . keep moving . . . and hope one day it will get lost for good! What can I say? We all have our little eccentricities and flaws, right?
    Stop looking at me that way! You may think you don't. You may think those creams you ordered online, and your visits to the dentist and eye doctor and ear doctor and witch doctor and psychiatrist and cryptozoologist have transformed you into the picture of perfection and health. Well, I'm here to say otherwise! Okay, okay, I'm here to say something else. Or maybe I'm just here for no intents and purpose. Perhaps this entire introduction is entirely unintentional. A mere beforethought of a changed mind.

Like wind whistling through your ears. It could be a bad dream, because you dozed off as soon as you opened this book. Not that I'm implying the book is boring or anything. That's for you to decide. In my opinion, it is quite the opposite.

What we have here, as we hover on the brink of madness, are some of the most strange and psychotic poems of a mind adrift. Reading them can only be described as pulling your brain inside out, then tying it in a bow like a pretzel and drop-kicking it into a gorge, a very deep gorge, where it will be washed by a stream of consciousness toward the outer limits and beyond. Well, that was my experience. Yours could be different. That's the thing about poetry. The lines can be interpreted, like art, especially abstract art, in various ways. And when your brain is a little off, a little twisted to begin with . . . even better!

Yet from the very first lines, it is clear the man whose mind drifts amidst the haze of deluded perspectives is indeed an artist with words. At times he strips them bare, down to the bone, revealing the gory details, or the heart that flutters and pounds within. A poet scribbling thoughts on napkins while frequenting a soup kitchen that we are invited to read between bites and scoops of breakfast.

With each page it becomes evident this is not a book of random pieces, but rather the pieces of a jigsaw puzzle, for we quickly see that there is cohesion, connection. It seems more like an off-the-cuff literary novel, literally penned in verse and the occasional prose passage, rather than a collection of poems. We can glimpse fragments of life through the eyes of the dysfunctional poet, as well as the stories of those whose lives he observes or shares or takes. It is both a fascinating and disturbing view of humanity, of reality in every gruesomely vivid detail, or the distorted reflections on a spoon. As we decipher the story of this poet whose writings verge upon the bizarre, we must venture "out there" to the fringes of sanity where the freaks and the cantaloupe play.

You might wish to consult a doctor before embarking on the trip. I say this with all sincerity, despite not trusting doctors much myself. Consider yourselves warned (or self, in case you do not hear voices).

Don't take it from me. Seriously, this is my copy. Get your own and read it, and then everything I've said will sink in like a stone. Or your brain could spill out of your ears, I don't know. That probably only happened once or twice. Practically everything has side effects if you read the fine print. My advice, don't read the fine print. You'll sleep better at night. Or in the daylight hours if you're like me and can't seem to go to bed when you're supposed to.

(Disclaimer: I am not responsible for any adverse reactions to the reading of this book since I did not write it, so please blame Vincenzo and quit calling me! That wasn't you? Well, I don't answer the phone anyway.)

~ Lori R. Lopez

Author of *Chocolate-Covered Eyes*
*Out-Of-Mind Experiences*
*An Ill Wind Blows*
*Poetic Reflections* (a poetry column and book series)
*The Macabre Mind Of Lori R. Lopez*
*Dance Of The Chupacabras*
*The Fairy Fly* and more

# CHAPTER ONE

## The Distance Between Two Worlds

## 7:00 A.M. Windows

"The kind of city that makes your nostrils burn."
Detroit old man,
smells like delirium and sewage.

Here I once thought, or perhaps I think again, somewhere in time:
    A neat kind of madness
    all wrapped in a blanket on a stairwell,
        (flaking rust, even the ruins know how to die).

Cigarette smolders in the ashtray.

    As the world burns I burn out—
    atmospheres layered in smoke-stacked disenchantment.

Nightmare man, nightmare man, yet another nightmare, man
    can't say I didn't warn you.

I don't know myself when I awaken,

at the wheel of time,
my eyes like black holes
the mirrors chide but never lie.

Those aren't my fingers
    that tremble and shake.
Oh,
and I almost forgot:
There isn't a sun to rise today.
Never could tell that it might be summer.
    August you have been cruel to me

# VINCENZO BILOF

with this sweat I pass unto thee fire and welfare.
The state thereof.
No furniture, just a bullet hole in the window across the street.
No cars pass in the pretend silence.

    (Whisper it again.
    Nothings repeated across the quilted patterns
    of someone else's tomorrow.
    Whisper it again.)

    All the blood when I close my eyes.

Visit the diner where a martyr washes dishes
with soup-stained fingers, a brunette
wearing an apron instead of a virginal veil.
They never told her college isn't
for everyone.
Just those who needed to
sleep in playgrounds

could
use
a good breakfast.

# Motorcyclical

Been here
before. Maybe on blank pages,
staring, on a window sill
looking at a brick painting.

"Years ago," he sounds like
a pirate chewing rubber
bands. White hair curls
in mud on strong shoulders.
"Feeling better
this morning?"

His home is made in shadow,
teeth carved from cement blocks,
a metal drum full of fire
while the August sun is resurrected.

"I know you?" I nod, because homeless
men enjoy the solitude of their madness,
and I don't know how
I know this.

"I'm the last one left. From the old
crew. Thought I wouldn't recognize ya.
We talked 'bout this yesterday, and
last Toosday."

He winked. "Brain and intestine
noodle soup. I'll never forget that
day. You showed us
a trick or two. And she loved you
for it. I'll never forget her name.

# VINCENZO BILOF

Talk about it ever' time. Good
to have you back. Ain't had soup
since that last night. You turned
    us into prophets. Yeah. HE HE HE HE HE HE HE."
    We were here yesterday.

## Eye Stains

"Halt! Who goes . . . ?"

A blind man asks mightily, oh haughtily
       pause and cough, don't get caught.
These eyes;
look at all these
eyes, forgive me and the depths of my twisted imagination,
sometimes I know not

where I must go.

I eat here over the cracked cement, the blank cement, the
cracked cement
       if I put my ear to the ground it might be burnt, the
flames *here*

*in this city burn forever.*
Going to try again today,
Never say die attitude oh, I said it

                                                                               Die.

But that would be so easy and I can't OMIT---—-agree with you more,

every step
along the broken path brings me here to this place
where I might consider a promise or two.

You must wonder at my mystery.

# VINCENZO BILOF

I sit here and wait for your glances.
Pouring the coffee.
The apron.

Brunette apocalypse upon the threshold of decades

the lashes falling for the Christ who weeps
and begs for the sins you design.

Oh,
I am here, I want to announce . . .

Look at me, look at me:
      A wretch like me not like you.
      (we are again, consider it a lesson learned, another
lesson to be sought, another

thing

      to teach you

only wounds you deeply)
Can't imagine another human emotion besides fear.

# Pretty Girls

Beside the silverware
is a pen.

Maybe it wants me to speak.

A television with glass eyes,
leather-ripped seats
smoky kitchen,

two young men sharing hangover dreams
would look more

whole
without their arms

Lorraine has long eyelashes,
the pen wants to bleed

here I am. This might be me.

Bulging flesh of pock-faced
mother, apron stained dawns
the routine, staple breasts

into eyes. Chef pokes head
could his beard

melt, industrial acid bath
cars remember how to park outside.

# Casual Ruinations

"Tell those damn liars who have declared that aint aint a word and neither does it require
Apostrophe.

Listen to this, I mean, wait, I know it sounds redundant but there . . .
okay, your lips are either snarling or smiling,
so should I laugh or cry?

Sure, it matters.

As I was saying.

The word is rather rebellious because the language-owners have ignored
that the word has a common usage and common understanding.

Fits the lexicon and it's there for you to deny."

(Maybe I should say

call it a curse word for the unwashed, they can have it
like the blood on this counter mirrored in yellow light, like mustard
and ketchup could never stain oblivious.)

"Eggs and ham would be nice, Lorraine."
I hide from emerald eyes,
pretend to watch the dusty men
      the toothless men

rape cell phones with fingers
souls sucked into screens.

# THE HORROR SHOW

"Commit yourself to
a code you're afraid

to violate." A plate shatters and eyes stick to fragments from
vein-laden skulls.

In my nightmares I have seen the dead flesh of heroes melted hot
over a rusty grille.

"Sizzle baby sizzle."
This counter finger-painted in shades of blood or memory.

My nightmares lived so much reality.
Everything I see reminds me of something horrible I've seen before
like I've lived another life or my memory is damaged. Am
 speaking to you now?

> "Could be damaged."
> What sane man would choose the life of a drifter haunted by
> dreams, "could get cash from doctors
> Volunteer lab rat maybe there's a cure"
>
> Laugh that up, no cure for the difference;
> you are what you eat; you're a man now stand up.
>
> Could be damaged
> "Don't recall ever having job skills, go to school young man
> you're smart,
> the jobs will just come to you, it's true,
>
> could be damaged."

Messages in code printed upon a napkin.
"Do you save your poems to a computer?"
she asked, or asks.

I can't remember waking up to one or another.
"Is this a part of your process?"

**VINCENZO BILOF**

# An Intimate Confessional

You can hear me.
There is remembrance. Cognition.

The silence which follows catharsis.
Shared pieces of a child's puzzle.

I'm the boy in the passenger seat with the winter cap,
the big bulky coat, you know the type. With mittens.

The only color is gray. A thunderstorm gray which soaks the
brick and the vinyl, the bright cars, a collective gasp.

A hole in the sky spreads apart the blank expression,
here is nothing to hear. Coiling, an exiled funnel cloud

shades of future. A teenager in the house. *Beep beep beep.
Beep beep beep.*

A blue band filled with yellow letters scrolls the warning.
The end of the world has a scream to share

so get the cats into the basement. Cover your heads.
"Why are they still upstairs?" my sister can't reply,

mouth frozen. Next time we close the screen door
we know how to avoid the lightning paths,

freeways lurch and the cement of years yawns
"everything will be okay" is the authoritative

## THE HORROR SHOW

meltdown. Jet flight shred the afternoon, jet-black sky
as nature shares its idea of vengeance

coiling again, swirling.

# VINCENZO BILOF

## When She Needs Herself

The corners of your mouth twitching between frown and smile.
"Haven't decided which face the world deserves to see today?"

"What's that supposed to mean?"

"Ain't s'pposed to mean nuthin."

Rebels the words I could speak with my eyes
we invent our own language.

Desperate at the incoming life.
The possible dream, the common dream

"the works," shall we say, ahem, allow me to clear this passage
                                        A moment of silence for
the words

"Mighty fine shoes, Lorraine."

"Never heard that before out of a straight man."
We're up on our haunches and circling.

"Your breakfast."

Last year's dreams met here
because she smirks and wants to walk away,
instead she smirks and tilts her head,

"Don't fall asleep on me again . . . "
That's how a promise explodes into starlight.

# THE HORROR SHOW

## Caged-Tunnel Lucidity

A desert, an outspoken desert.
Cry for all of the angels
who have descended upon this plain
the illusion of grass might
*Flourish.*

This is rust or blood,
bricks touched by flame and
vomit,

      flies sleep in eardrums
a train grinds upon the tracks
but there is no train
there are no tracks

I know about dead bodies
in garbage bags
and nobody wants to look,

    *Hey, Dad, why don't these men have a home?*
    *Aren't they cold?*
    *Danny, don't ask your father such questions,*
    *can't you see he's writing behind*
    *his sunglasses?*

where no worm feeds upon remains
because there are no worms
or there are no remains to bring the worms.

                                                     (Crave

the imminent disaster)

# VINCENZO BILOF

Why do windows bleed,
is it because of the invisible train
shakes the red verse?

> *Doctor, if we left he wouldn't know*
> *how to miss us.*
>  *Constantia, I know.*
> *Let me hold you.*

here,
the moon squats
low.
"Man, you have something to say to me,"

This man wearing a golden pocket watch and
cowboy hat, ask him the time.
Rabbit, rabbit, tell me there isn't enough time.
He opens his mouth to advertise his abyss.
Blood spills like a waterfall from his cavernous mouth
locusts dance haphazardly

before his eyes.

Among the buildings
we are parched, throats
clenched, birds breaking
their wings
before the train arrives
grinding,

> *Grandma said you ran away from home?*
> *Is that true, Dad?*

I knew these people, once.

# Time Unknown

        Wiping sleep from my eyes.

Lorraine, sitting in chair before a window with the blinds drawn over.
Supplicant, those smooth, careful hands.
"You passed out," she said.

I told her it wasn't the first time, and
it wouldn't be the last.

"You hit your head," she said.

A picture of a policeman and a little girl,
Saint Lorraine,
destined for soup kitchens
and diners.

"Why did you bring me here?"
To her place, a private realm,
an invitation.

"You've been here before."
The picture belongs on a mural
or a museum.

"We've had this conversation before, too,"
I stare at the picture. "You
know what I'll say,
what I'll ask."

An uncomfortable shift, her girlish
face tilting, watching me.

# THE HORROR SHOW

"You fall asleep all the time. Doctor Humphrey
came into the restaurant one day, said he was looking for you and that
he knew you came in all the time. He said you were dangerous.
We talked, and I
decided to help you.
Protect you
Give you money."

She's not a stranger,
a woman designed
by my words,
perhaps,
if I knew my name,
I would whisper hers
just to hear the sigh,
because this is all for her,
not me.

Saint Lorraine, my guardian
keeps me in the cage,
I'm being studied
rather than saved,
researched rather than
housed.

    Amnesia, narcolepsy,
wandering, wandering,
this is the horror I wake up to
this is the horror that hides
in the sun at daybreak
or breeds in the cracks
or washes on the shore
with pop cans and beer
bottles and cigarettes
and diapers and fingernails
and it wanders,
wanders.

# VINCENZO BILOF

              (Even her mumbling seems trite
                        she cranes her head to peer through
blinds,)

"I want to remember you."
Her eyes blinked at my words

before she said, "I don't have to be
                at the soup kitchen, they won't miss me tonight
                I can take care of you. You remember my name, you've
                seen me working at the kitchen,
                visited me. I want to help. You're sick
                and I—"

"Have you called him?"
(Why are you running away? You are different,
your nightmares hold sway over you.
       She didn't say.)

What we hear is not what we think.
What we hear or what we see is not the ruination.

*Everything becomes blurred.*

# An Honest Review

Outside, I see an octopus on each face.

That's not the sound of my head exploding,
the critics have spoken, arbiters of the just,
the garbage handlers of the universe.

I hear them, even now.        (The octopus glares)
Hold my hand while I wither and drown,
slip into the sewer where the
dead dreams of artists reside.

I was famous? A popular man?
Hiding from the scourge
feels safer. To whom do I pay for

(irony cracks the glass where windows hide)

these kind words?

Why do I
        *you agreed to a review*
        *I wonder what she thinks*
        *what if she only gives me two stars*
        *my rankings*
        *my sales*
        *my*
        *how do I please thee*
        *you didn't understand and I have to pay*
        *you didn't understand and I have to pay*

suction into waves

**VINCENZO BILOF**

# Echoes of a Child's Mirage

Outside,
through the blinds,
a man wavers in the street,

*we are the blank spaces,*
*can you hear us calling?*
*we are the dread and the sorrow.*

(Lorraine speaks of her father)

*Dear author,*
*I'm a fan of your work.*

(Lorraine suggests my
 memory can return. All I have is her.

Something about soup kitchens. Words scattered
across a multiverse.)

*Dear Mr. Award-Winning Poet,*
*can you not hear the cheers?*
*Dear Mr. Million-Dollar Man,*
*your soul is delicious.*

(Lorraine mentions that I once wrote her a poem

about what brain tastes like if you add soup broth into the skull.

Warm brother, of course. She asks if I'm interested in trying it
sometimes. She says she'll do anything with me if it means we can be
together.)

*Dear Mr. Immortal, I want to open
my wrists and
let your words squirm into my veins.*

(Lorraine asks if she can spend the night with me because
she thinks it will help, considering she's "helped me out" a few times.
She says I prefer it that way.)

*Dear Mr. Zero,
I want to sleep with your words.*

(Lorraine suggests my memory will return if I kill enough people.
She says she'll do anything in the name of a greater cause. I don't know
what she understands to be greater.)

poised lazily over a crack in the pavement,
his head rolls between his shoulders.
He won't move out of the street.
I've seen this before.

Now I can think about what it's like to be afraid to know myself,
or not know anyone besides myself,
or know not what I am inside of her,
or anyone else I have seen or felt,
or needed or dreamt of,
or bled for.

# Awake

Someone should tell me where I can find my illusion.
I'm a knife's edge dancer poised

hurt you like I need

all answers reside in the number which signifies nothing.
Call it coming full circle.

Sleep beneath the pendulum soaked in memory who I am
overrated.

# Other Women

"Well I'm not anything
like them. I don't feel
anything, except
the eyes of other men,
on me, all
on me.

You're in another
world, somewhere
in your head
where nobody
can touch, a place
full of black spider
webs.

You're famous, you
know. Fans have been
looking for you, a
screaming legend
hiding in a soup
kitchen.

      You don't remember
      Constantia, or Danny?
      They're missing, too.
      She couldn't help you,
      I mean, your wife.

That's what happened
to you. She didn't
know

you or appreciate
you.
But I'm here,
and if I can bring you
back from the eclipse,
I can help save
thousands of people,
and that's worth my life.

    Take me for the future."

                Reaching for Blades


I remember that I don't
remember. Afflicted
and suffering, drowning
and burning.

Words orbit images
saturated in azure
cut through by fingers,
falling, slipping, falling.

Echoes of a woman's voice,
a name somewhere,
a boy's bright eyes
clothed in adjectives.
Mourning, maybe.

Lorraine the traitor,
an octopus gripping secrets.
Somebody knows my name
or the magnetism
of bright computer screens

                        with electrode surge
                        shocking fingers to life.

# THE HORROR SHOW

                    I used to remember me

without falling asleep.

If Lorraine bleeds I
can find the secret; in
                    the wet, red slime I will
                    see the face of another

woman and a boy.

It makes sense to me:
she sacrifices her life
every day to hear
murdered silences from
the cracked lips of skeletons
who're already dead.

I've heard a blade
slide into flesh
and touch the edge of bone.
Sounds like the alphabet
return from memory's grave.

I don't know who I was but there's an idea;
I might be what I'll try
to become, otherwise
she'll just bleed a lot.

# VINCENZO BILOF

# We Boldly Go to Nowhere

"I'm a poet," I whisper into her ear.

My hand closes nicely around her neck. Her eyes don't widen as I would have expected them to. I want to see her lips part gently so that she might gasp for breath. A tendril of hair curls around the curves of her ear. I know she has been expecting this from me and I don't know why. I know she wants this from me and I don't know why.

I straddle her and push her onto the threadbare carpet. Her eyes close and I realize how young she is. She is young and living alone here in the city where rust is the color of blood and blood is the color that the homeless wear on the street and rust is the color that reminds us that we are mortal. To be nineteen again, not that I remember. To love as you have loved, Lorraine, and to love as you still want to know love.

My hands tightly applying pressure, squeezing her to sleepiness, I lean down and kiss her tight, bulging lips. Spittle is not the same as saliva. Her eyes now widen and I think there is a question in them. I don't know if an answer will provide any sort of satisfaction to anyone who cares to observe. The good doctor once said that I take pleasure in dealing pain, but I can't remember his face and I can't remember that he really said it at all, only that I believe that he said it, which is good enough.

"There is no cure for *me*," I explain.

Lorraine, you are a project of mine, dearest. You came here because you maintain an accurate disclaimer of loneliness. I can't wait to show you what my heart looks like, which would necessitate that I show you what yours looks like, too. It's only fair.

"I'm in love with you," I say while her eyes roll backwards into her skull.

# CHAPTER TWO (YEARS AGO)

## Affairs in Order

## THE HORROR SHOW

# Catholic Homicide

Constantia sat on the edge of the bed,
rubbing the back of her neck,
staring at the night glow
through silk drapers imported
from Rome.

The doctor watched the specimen
arch her back. He sighed
and smiled.

Her profile locked in place.
        "I loved him, once."

Doctor Humphrey sat up.
        "I don't regret this."

A smirk complained on her lips.
        "Because you love him, too.
        you're obsessed.
        His damnation, his insanity.
        Why won't you let me
        ock him away?"

The doctor massaged her shoulders.
There was so much she couldn't understand.
An opportunity
to save the world, in addition to
an immortal soul.

Now was the perfect time to share
the lie she anticipated,

a lie for the flesh.
> "He's too important.
> He's not aware that he doesn't exist.
> You made him happy,
> maybe you even changed
> him, for a bit. But you went
> along with the ghostwriting
> idea . . . you and your love
> for poetry, for art."

She threw her head back
and laughed for the sake
of monsters and warriors,
crucified prophets dangling
years from their feet.
> "Meanwhile, we let him
> walk around in a stupor,
> kill women, and bury
> them in garbage bags?
> You can't understand him,
> Doctor. Fucking me
> won't bring his
> reflection into focus.
> My husband will kill me,
> and our son.
> That's really
> what you're dying to see."

A critical moment in moonlight
or the glow of somewhere else
envisioned, paradise,
lovers and fathers, children
with dirty faces and bright eyes,
the birth of love.
> "Nobody misses these women,
> you won't be alone,
> I'm here.
> I'll protect you. Do you

# THE HORROR SHOW

    want him to
    hurt you?"

Eyelids flicker or implode,
a necklace upon her throat
unnoticed by her husband
because her husband
might be dead.
        "Keeping him close,
        I've been . . . in denial . . .
        I didn't want to lose him . . .
        say it. Say it now. The truth."

A man of science listens
for brains that squirm,
the widow of a living poet
has skin that shines
in memory, or
in labyrinths
    "You've been selfish.
    Used his name, his
    worlds, his fingers.
    You showed him
    how to fade into
    the idea of oblivion.
    Even this—selfish."

Agree-upon

silences weigh            the                stones

of years.

The fate of a poet
whose heart walks on water.

## Sepia Tonal

Plotlines.

Rising chests, fall, resolve

        The evidence, the sacrifice.
        Herein this scrap book
        lies the origins

Exposition denies setting
temples or churches,

        angles
        portraits of glass

headlines in black
scraps, litter and stain white

        the father
        placed his boy and wife
        in the basement

(it's a tornado, a storyteller might impart)

a train
beyond the houses

        the boy became

without a father who stood on the porch

shards (of
        rain).

**THE HORROR SHOW**

## Dirt Roads, Snake Pits

We fell in love
because he knew me
over tears
and dried breakfasts
an apartment filled to the brim
with pop bottles
ten cent deposit

nights on the balcony
telling our hearts we were right
hail made him shiver
thunder made his nose bleed

cold sweats when the train passed
but we remained, animate,
murderous against
reason

the heresy of need
inflicting each other with
fantasies chasing shadows

movie theaters with cum
on the upholstery, ripped
our clothes
devoured organisms

us, just us, until he said
the words that
killed us both

## VINCENZO BILOF

sharing a poem is like fucking
a Muslim, Jew, atheist
scientist
bitch
whore,
pig
heretic
heretic
Mormon
sociopath
rock star with lusts straight from
the mouth of Socrates

it was perfect
until I woke up
and he didn't remember
and I knew

he was a killer
and I was him.

## We Can Be Metaphors

The doctor opened his pen
a woman wept

years ago a cat yawned
another woman wept
surfaces of tide

some oceans forget they exist
paint her, or listen

associate
        with

                murder

a boy was drowned in loud noises
by his mother

let him become a poet
      and get lost in alleys
      with dead people
      in his arms

the doctor could feel his eyelashes
drop
the pen

morality surrendered to marriage
the doctor lost a woman
to see a woman
lose herself

resurrect herself
hold herself
ask why she had to be wrong
for the sake of art

which is never

                              really

(her name
whispers itself)

or on a gravestone
parents have wept

           a father in a tornado
           lost
           the train survived

faith in life
dead girls are out there

years ago a cat stretched
and here
a woman weeps
           immortality
           slithers

*Constantia.*

**THE HORROR SHOW**

# Nous Faisons Tout pour l'Amour

He never wanted us to be tragic
behind my ribcage there are bones
on fire, but it's not rage
I feel for him

Suffering years in the illusion
of love or family,
when nothing is real
except for hurt,
Danny . . . I . . . he's a good son

What I've done
What I've needed

truth is worse than horror
yourself, skinless

naked in the snow
glaciers for eyes

I'll confess again
your smile belongs to
a skeleton

last time, you turned
from the computer
your underwear around your ankles
and laughed

when I told you the doctor is
watching you kill people

# VINCENZO BILOF

and so am I

you asked where the milk was.

I'll write it down once and for
all and
let you peer into the truth
and you can see,
yes,
you are not.

                        Sols

The two poets
watched the town bleed in the sunrise

"How much do you love me?"
                        he asked.

The dead woman,
a beggar,
looked like she was sleeping,

Constantia grasped
for meaning in transcendence
a dawn that belonged to them

                    "I want to be caught, maybe,"
                    poised on his heels
                    as if he might leap
                    over the roof
                    and hop into the clouds
                    and wave goodbye

There were no seconds
without him,
time had already died
futures paused.

# THE HORROR SHOW

"What will you do next?"
                        she whispered
                        the famous question
                        she never dared
                        to mouth.

He began to saw away
at the beggar's fingers
with a butter knife.
A dog eagerly licking its paws
makes the same sound.

The poet worked and worked,
then stood and hurled the digits
at the sky. They fell
like stones.

"Now you know who I am!"
                        The poet walked along
                        the edge of the roof.

Constantia wanted to look at the sun.

"My mother used to play loud music,
to get me to sleep after my father was swallowed
by a storm," the poet danced.

There was blood
in his words,
a romance of truths
nobody wanted

martyrs for the sake of art,
he would throw it in her face.

"We'll ghostwrite," was her final reply.

# CHAPTER THREE (Lorraine)
## The Grand Experiment

## Reactionaries

Compelled, drawn.

Here. I am.

Watching a beast salivate, pace, wonder.
                               Claws clacking
on the floor of a cage.
I'm supposed to point
and make a mundane
remark to a stranger.

"The doctor told me you hurt."
There's nothing for him to say.

Addicted to suffering
and from here I can watch
him rip his own face off while
crying. But I'm here for him instead,
a sculpture of a dead
metaphor.

This isn't personal,
and I should be afraid. My first
day behind

the counter

or in the soup kitchen, hungry eyes

                           undressed years
and saw a little girl

(I know because they told me), "Lorraine's

a pretty name I think
your bottom lip should quiver."

Fear can be someone else's god,
dog-eared and stuttering.

I didn't need to be this man's mother;
he never buried the people
he murdered because he can't
remember them.
        His memory was stolen
        while he slept.

## THE HORROR SHOW

# The Questions a Madwoman Might Ask

The doctor will help save the world by curing madness. "Cure madness to cure evil." Cold rooms and light upon spectacles to render eyes invisible. A charitable woman. The entropy of poverty. Policemen nodding their heads at the chalk outlines of children. Light peering through the holes in windows where bullets have flown. "I can cure evil by falling in love."

The doctor nodded his head and nearly grinned. A slumbering poet who murdered his family holds the enzymes in his brain that can save the poor before they're forced to fight another war; there will be life after death. "I need you."

Don't render unto me the nightmares of a martyr. The thieves and idolaters peer at me over their soup bowls and consume my flesh without my name. The poet doesn't know his own soul. "It's not about the money."

It's not about the money. Let me show you pictures of his wife and child. The salesman attempts to play the harp with broken fingers. "I want to see the dead."

Maggots writhe upon vomit-encrusted blankets and you speak of madness and its cure. Salvation comes in many colors, a rainbow of amber, red, white, and glass. Mouths drowning in the rainbow, livers reliant upon pain and sorrow to feed the disease. And you call it madness. "He loved them dearly."

Narcoleptic afflictions reflected in misplaced organs. Edgar Allan Poe was buried alive. We believe in archetypes, the designs of exposed ribcages and eyelids forever closed. A woman and a child not bound would have screamed for ages. Life betrays love and love betrays the sanctuary of Mondays and Tuesdays. I'm familiar with his swirling eyes and I have swallowed the oasis.

A thousand messiahs would be proud of me. The doctor has given him money to live and I am the catharsis, the expendable victim of philanthropy soaked in greed.

I am like an addict staring over the edge of a cliff where everything I need has fallen over that edge and into a clouded valley

there is something
I think something.

## THE HORROR SHOW

# This Feeling for You

This apocalypse somewhat obstinate.
Close my mouth and the mind is left
to the sorrow of a hermit.

Injected, the tears of the world seep
into warm blood;
the humility of a nun, so they tell me.

Strangers from the midnight soup kitchens
the child-like shadows
manipulating, violence-soaked dark.

Saving lives with a smile and a ladle,
herein slumbers the man who
murdered my father

chest cavity exposed by the blades
which no longer weep. Officer down,
choking on his last breath. Daddy Daddy

why can't I see him? The coffin has closed.
A revolving planet                                          (The
superhero's dream has returned)
where the damned can be loved.

Your words contain the end of the world;
in my arms you would be immortal.
I'm not ready to die.

Styx feeds the dam, a monument of
Lorraine, blood or fire licking edges
cursed by my need for you.

# VINCENZO BILOF

A woman in love sees something absolute and nameless;
trangers abandoned on the rings of Saturn
provoke the quivering universe.

## Hanged by a Thread

You didn't hear me when I said I knew your name
A moment of inertia
Timeless, you eye your plate
There is naught but silence in a loud world
You said that when you looked out of your window in the morning

      You noticed the cement
      Had a hole in it
You didn't know me when I gave the bill
I have a secret
There was a pause between us and you knew I needed to talk
The doctor said that
      You're dangerous
      A hazard to yourself
      You've killed your wife
      Only you don't know that
      You had a wife at all
It changes nothing
Words set aside for tomorrow
Was that silence so deadly to her
I am left to wonder.

**VINCENZO BILOF**

# The Invisible Treatise

This road drowns you

beseech the moment and hold tight the man
       with no demands
*(makes his*
*return,*

*and turns)*

a man fallen asleep as if raw sex brought him down
felled him                                       laid him low.

I'll wait here and stare at the wounded sky
blue night bleeds onto the world
now required to need you, a promise I made

in memoriam:

"These shoes don't fit, Daddy."

My father tousled my hair, said goodnight,
and left
us.

# Law Giver

Waited for
the moment
defined
by histories.

*(Those hands were always warm)*
The poet sleeps while
I wait, bound.

"Why do you do it?" I asked
Daddy, once, years

ago.
"Monsters don't know

they're monsters."

        His hands were
        on the wheel,
        like they used to be
        on the small of my back
        when the wheels came
        off, "Wheeeeeecc!"
        Those hands were always warm.
"Save them
from themselves," Daddy
smiled. Trees passed.

He patted my thigh
with his warm hand.
A smile breaking his jaw.

# VINCENZO BILOF

"Monsters want to be
like you and I, but they
don't know how."

      A dragon on parole,
      released from the iron castle,
      removed the top of Daddy's
      head with scissors,
      propped open his chest
      with Coke bottles
      ten of them, five on each
      side,
      paper clips
      holding up
      flesh,
      making a neat little tent.

I saw pictures, later,
and remembered
Daddy's warm hands.

# Love Song Written for the Amnesiac

I want to tell him the truth,
just to stop his heart from setting the world aflame.

I am here, gagged and bound;
I have given myself to a madness
that has a name but not a memory

    a name for madness.
    I.

Whosoever dreamt of this prison
finds me shattered
and withdrawn,
my legs crossed,
a church girl who needed
revulsion, not love

beaten and broken.

I've got a tragic poet for you:
a family man
kills whatever a family can
the ticking of a slow clock
and all the light fades
consider the sun
like I

have marble eyes
so useless
confessions can be written in dramatic form

damnation will make me beautiful
doctor, you promised
medical man medical man
cures whatever a madman can

if I could play the violin it would sound like this:

*tears and tears and tears*
*flow like a river*
*collected the timeless tributary*
*under a broad*
*pink sun*
*that dies at the hands of a slow summer evening*
*and all things are naturally timeless*
*the river cannot be saved*

the violin would break, there.

**THE HORROR SHOW**

# Love Song Written for the Narcoleptic

Poems like pictures cannot find their conclusions for they do not exist
I watch you dream and I watch you slumber

while away the hours

Oh so slowly your eyelids dance and shiver like your hand, a hand that has played the piano of words strung across the eternal alphabet of concepts rendered meaningless by the translations of ancient orators, all of whom knew the truth, yes, some truth that horror is the path to righteousness and I have loved your words while my cold legs dangled beneath a fragile desk while the teacher clamored for attention, all things yes all things, all words, yes all words, yes, and I think that yes, a romance best left to rest, an idea that all men die alone and I think about watching you undress all dreams with your words.

## Love Song Written for the Poet

(What else is there to say
I will await the hour of reckoning with the patience of a saint
I know that I will pay
his fingers

rush over my spine with a rapist's taint
Let me speak and proclaim the day
Lay me down, lay me down, for the hour grows late).

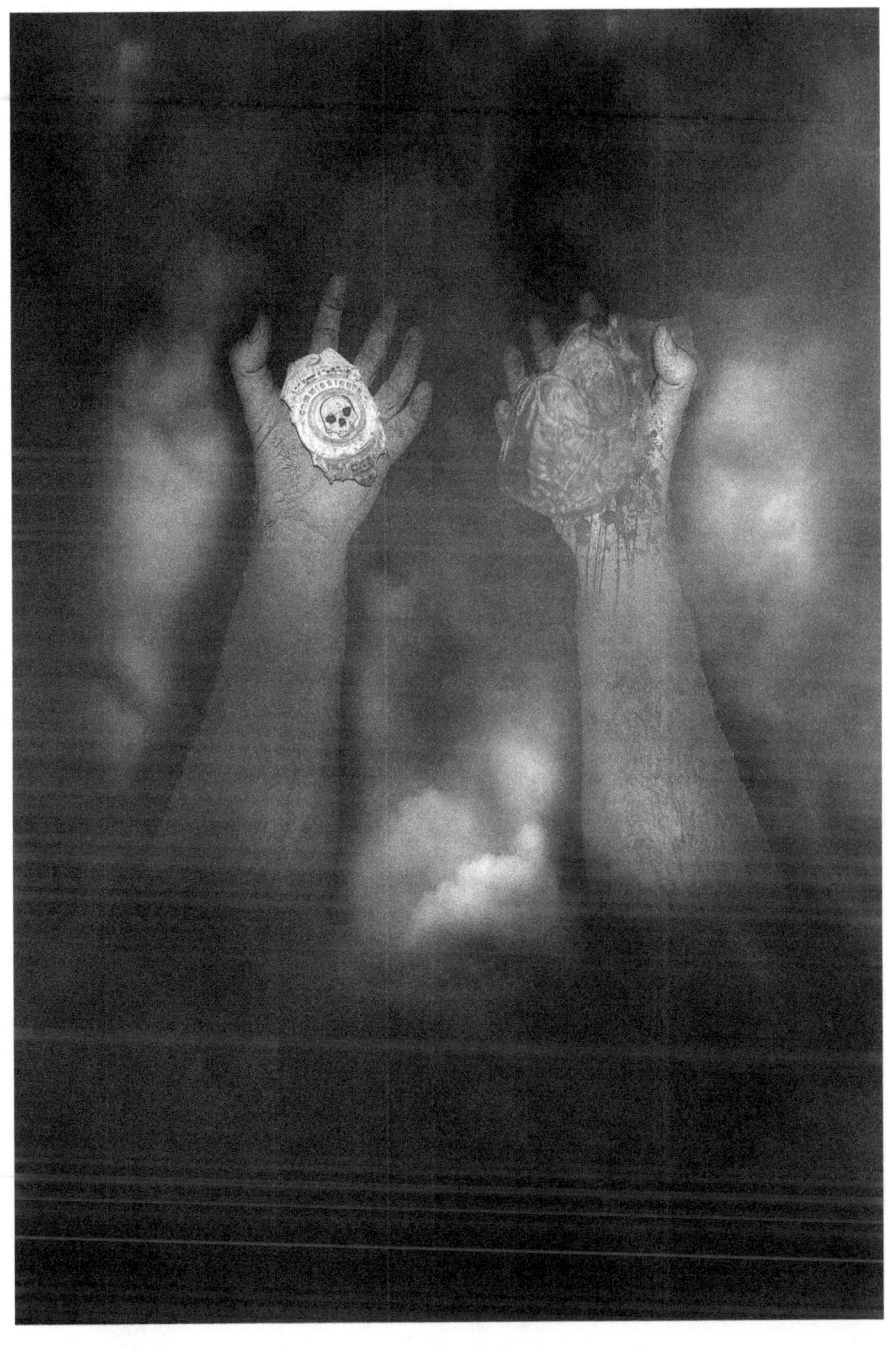

# CHAPTER FOUR (The Doctor)
## Hippocrates Weeps

## Words of Advice

I don't think one must die for love.

I may have studied medicine and spent years
      toiling, smiling, projecting, diagnosing.

I may have married the first woman who decided
      I'm a safe bet for all my education, the money
      I'd make

and
      the children, think of the children unborn and wrapped
 a dream.
Screwing, lying, arguing,
the years
oh, the years.

A man is not made to kill what he loves so none other may share in the secrets
I tell you a man is not mad.

Believe me, I know
nothing is simpler than love.

## Common Diagnosis

The specter leans in to listen.

(The doctor sets his glass of beer down upon the bar and wipes his mouth with the back of his sleeve and mumbles something that borders on incoherence, and the mutterings of a madman whose language is known only to him or an alien). "Okay, maybe I made a mistake or two

along the way."
There seems to be a silence which empties out of the happy-hour crowd.
Men have never needed a bleak box to serve as a confessional
"I loved her, too. I mean, his wife was positively beautiful

and she told me never to give up on him. I did it all for her."

And if you listen closely there's the hum of a television,
another Detroit sports team takes its time losing,
the walls are stained by the cigarettes of yesterday;
a burn that no longer suffices. "I've always done what's in the best interests . . ."

He's going to say it. He's really going to say it and he's ashamed.
"He should've been locked up long ago. But it isn't my place to be right about things." He doesn't want to lie now

no deductible can cover a lie

raise your right hand and share the oath once again treat them all and treat them well
save the world with a handshake and a stethoscope

refer a man to another man

# THE HORROR SHOW

refer a woman to another man share a drink good doctor on your boat
hide behind a fence and buy your wife a garden

water the lawn and pick up the dog shit

pick up the kids from school
drive around and wear a smile when your tools are at rest
your tools should never rest

whose oath did you take
the bar screams out against the windows of light with mute lusts
waitress wearing black pants
young, maybe going to college

"I know I did my best, damn it. The best interests of science. A greater good. I didn't do it for the money. I have enough. No man should ever have enough. No man should ever serve a greater good. It requires the sacrifice of one's soul. Don't tell me

I could've saved their lives."

this is what failure feels like: satellites crashing
onto the surface of the moon
debris orbits the stars in cold disdain for theory
squeezing enzymes through patterns
nothing stifled, nothing. "But, I told her it was dangerous when
she fell in love with me but oh, ugh, she is, she is."

(Waitresses slap their hands together in praise of a day which heralds the doom of youth but not the Vikings who died beneath a fountain with the languages of gods upon their lips; their cure for the human race was to live and to die.)

"We knew how he'd react. We knew all along."

## Free Money

Cash and
flow, brothers
in
arms, limbs, trembling
(once more

break apart) Romeo at the apothecary
wanted freedom
passions of the dead

illiterate thaumaturgy
a spell or two
yes
concrete suicide
a mentionable
(man, oh mortal

you are dust)
consideration unkind.

## Second Opinion

Skeletal the day
Half-
                                      cocked

death by love
suicide
*semper sic tyrannis*

                              burn                all

          lovers
wonder the children
prevent wars

uncareful tirades
icebox miracles and general confessions no drunkenness tells the story better

that's not
                                    a butterfly       but
it belongs to a family of born-again monarchs
mathematically inchoate

a drama shared between
sun and asteroid

burning hot burning bright burning forever burning and turning
burning and spewing
listen, consider it done
everything spins backward when it loves before it dies
mating calls and one breeding pit

# VINCENZO BILOF

                                            circle it all carefully
desecrate underpants

a score worth settling

                                  oh
nobody meant it that way

                     *primum non nocere*
        *(all dead languages should have their day in the sun)*

promises are fatal diseases
marriage
sign here, here, and here
all good things come in threes

"is there a doctor in the house?"
a silhouette stands and shouts
the cartoon drops dead prematurely

unlimited conversation
has a price only ten cents a minute

            ha ha ha ha ha ha ha ha ha ha ha ho ha ha ha ha
            ha ha
            ha
            ah

where does this stain belong
hemorrhage of the heart
a stroke of love
the dear old boy was strong

after all
the end

        is.

# The Disconsolate Opinion

There is hunger and then there is burning
a man who wakes up in the middle of a dream
can't find sleep in rain-drenched streets
nothing left for him

hands that have familiar
blood a man without
a wife lives without
a country

the disease remains incurable.

**VINCENZO BILOF**

# Searching for Shelly

This is the day we met:
My wife deserted me.
Said I was obsessed with
failure. Found myself in
a barroom. Everything
is cheap.

Sunglasses in a place
where light ends.
Colorless walls.

Sports cars driving
on oval-shaped cement
on the television screen.
Amber love in a glass.

A Sinatra song
echoes, wrinkled fingers
shake over the glass.
You smiled.
A show of bravado,
you asked if it was
because of a woman.

>Stranger, still.
>I asked if I was supposed
>to curse them all,
>if that was the right thing
>to do.

"That poem's been written before,"
was all you had to say.

# THE HORROR SHOW

Everything is ironic
when you're a doctor and you
can't save yourself.

"They're not mysteries,"
I should've laughed.
Pieces of them are
on the mind's highway,
memory paraphrases,
but you said something
clever.

        Rounds two and three.
        A shadow is perched behind
        tinted glasses.

Youth met us on the stools
and mocked our confessions.
Flesh made of melted chalk
on your cheeks, a vampire
who drained
words.

There was a name mentioned,
heard it before,
the resurrection of oratory
performance poetry.

        A necromancer who
        wanted his hand held
        by a woman who
        appeared for a fleeting
        moment, a woman
        who would say nothing
        involving words, eyes
        oding languages into stardust.

# VINCENZO BILOF

"That's what we're looking for,"
A moment of silence with
a stranger.

Rounds seven and eight went
missing. One of us mentioned

*Frankenstein.*

> A good idea in theory.
> Always looking for
> pieces to build a face
> but the face changes
> when we can't see.

Repeated highlights.
Swirling minutes
and my hands no longer
shook.
I wanted to ask if you thought
*Frankenstein* was
a healthy obsession.
I remembered who I was, though I couldn't recall
when last you spoke.

> I gave you my card.
> Neither one of us
> thought it awkward,
> because we both knew
> you would call me for help.

A year later you wrote a poem
about brothers and puzzles.

# THE HORROR SHOW

## Paid For

Pictures float by remaining
as they are. People who remember
how to smile. This
smells like inertia.
The horror of stasis,

nothing.

This is me years later.
Cure myself by curing
the poet.
More analysis, data-driven

directives.

Something doesn't move.
The television erupts, flat
or plasma, unknown origins
built on an alien planet
out of the severed hands
of Mr. Bossman's clients.

The

video is the replay.
Her name was Constantia,
not Connie. Married to the poet,
she sits with her hands folded
neatly upon her lap.

("He's already dead and I don't have

                              permission to
die.
I'm alone with a memory of a man,
he sits behind the sunglasses and
falls apart behind his office door
his eyes sucked into a computer screen.


He wasn't always like this"
       "I know.")

Gold hoop earrings;
he didn't mind when I bought them.
The poet rises,
a walking corpse,
moving across the floor toward
the podium. Time

echoes.

Hands like butterfly wings,
a tribute to
the country's hero.
His words have saved lives,
but he's not there

anymore.

("I don't know how I feel about
him winning the Nobel Prize. I used to
read his poems. You know him.
Your wife murdered your marriage.
Three people who are togethe
 alone. Why don't you
        fuck me
        when he's in his office,
            writing another prize-winner?")

# THE HORROR SHOW

His form eclipses
television light,
his lips are supposed to move,
where a speech is supposed
to reign,
silence races
to capture the audience,
a picture
of people who remember how to smile.

# The Science of Strangulation

Connie used to talk too damn
much; I'm the listener, a priest,
and I found the inside of her
because you were locked in
a crypt with a computer.

In the interests of science,
and because Connie and I agreed
maybe I should understand your
condition better,

I bought a pair of black gloves
and found a dirty old hag
in the same alley you
pissed in, and I wasn't
breathing, I mean, I was calm.
The whole time. I learned
something about myself, and you.

Strangling people took the fun out
of it, but your mind already believed
it before you started. Art
and sex are the same to you,
and Connie said your best
poems were written
when she pretended

to ignore your night
misadventures
the whole time, building crypts
with black gloves.

When Danny slept,
she was here with me, or we
watched you,
and saw. In the interests of science
and your wife's vagina.

# CHAPTER FIVE (The Poet)
## Words That Spell Rage

## THE HORROR SHOW

# Bile, Remembrances, Shards

The horrors one can inflict upon the mind
I don't know what else to say
      To whom does this damnation belong
      Easy-to-read portents
Consider me proper-fucked

I can hear the angels peeling off their wings
I write down the things that make sense
I write down the things that don't make sense
None of this makes sense

A married poet murders his wife
A bit of rage
      Pity the victim of madness
      Easy to tip-toe around the rim of the abyss
This story is fucked

I can feel the angels waiting to describe my sins to me
I wonder at my guilt
I wonder at all of the nightmares I have traversed
It all becomes clear to me

Words and monsters hold hands and dip their toes into crystal-clear water
Mirrored epitaphs of graffiti artists and prophets
      This city gave birth to me
      In the flame and the madness and the blood and the tears and
Dogs gang-fucking wet garbage cans

I can feel the angels writhe in agony as they kill themselves in

conspiratorial fashion
I know I have been abandoned
I know that my knees have bled from years spent in carefully-planned prayer-mode
I want to kill my wife again

The muse I seek lost in mirrors and sing-song screams
More truths spill out of a wide-open maw
    All evil remains nameless
    All music smells like death
God-fuck the English language and its myriad prisons

I can feel the angels logging on to live porn shows
I can identify the origin of humanity as a travesty
I can identify the rain of cigarette ash which pours out of this apocalypse
I want to kill you again

Oh holy triumvirate, evoke this longing for flesh
Watch my clothing collapse inward into heaps of dust
    Coleridge you harem-loving slime
    Wilde you hedonistic slob
All good poets fuck the devil in the mouth

I can feel the angels conversing about modern art
I bleed the lovely pain rendered unto years lost in bondage
I bleed because my wife had these large eyes that bulged out of her head
I know you want to witness this

One long road to Hell
One long road to some stupid tower or another
One long road to the short-end-of-the-stick
One long road out of life

Effervescent flavor-saving plastic-pink elephant in the shape of a mangled baby Jesus
Say it twice in Spanish not Latin all good languages die more

# THE HORROR SHOW

than once
Dear girl don't you know . . . know . . . know . . . what?
The manufactured woman on the cover of this magazine is
supposed to be you
Damn disappointment to the human race
You should be ashamed of your mask

Watch this spin and jump-kick
    Hold
        On
            To
                The
                    Capital
                        Letters

They don't have anywhere else to go
Wonder if you had something interesting to tell me
Perhaps over a cup of coffee and a cold breakfast you pretend to enjoy
No kiss on the first date
What good am I

Watch this spin and jump-kick
    That
        Is
            Your
                Stupid
                    Face
                      My
                          Dear
    Motherless whore-friend

Share what you've learned this evening about madness
It ain't what it used to be
HA HA HA HA HA
Ain't ain't ain't
I laugh at the one-thousand fractions-worth of apostrophes that hang
out in empty bars
Clamoring for the thunderous applause only the gentlemen own

# VINCENZO BILOF

Do I have an agent
Someone to perhaps represent me rape me destroy my artistic integrity
Use me sell me produce me advertise me
Sell me sell me sell me by the pound or by the word
Buy the word

Maybe not
Maybe or maybe not

Dig up the corpse of Baudelaire
See if he can show you how to care
Take a picture near Morrison's headstone
Eat the dead languages of lovely Ezra Pound

Every poet the adulterer
Every word is a crime
Ask Sylvia Plath and her wealthy husband
Some like it hot, after all
Every poet thinks that porn is a gift from Heaven
Every poet likes generalities
Every poet has fought in every war
In every way
Give them their flower power and ruin the American family with some new form of Suffrage
Thousands of years of inequality and we can change the world with a smile and a handshake
We can make it all better pay more reparations and celebrate
GREEN HISTORY MONTH
All you bastards and you sons-of-bitches
Listen to this derision
Every musician every cocaine-addict
Every sex junkie and video-game-playing slave
Every remote-controller-button-pushing-slave
Enjoy your commercials and Aristotle's plotlines
Enjoy all of the rip-off artists and the socialites
Wish upon a star the princess inherits an empire of hotels

I've heard that Jesus is black
Ask him if he has "SOUL" when you get to Heaven you racists
You scumbags you swine you you you eat this finger choke on it

Choke
On
It.

**VINCENZO BILOF**

# Past Tense

chameleons
eat
rabbit-disguises
killed
"Daddy
can
we
take
him
home
with
us?"

rather
eat
Mommy's
vaginal
corpse
idea

yes
idea

historical
murder
needs
wants
glass-rain
boxed-hearts oven-
baked

sadness
etched-in
sadness
pencils
scribbling inked-bones


remembrance
bodies
prone
minimalist-furniture-daydreams

gods
prophesized
bone-hieroglyphics
evidence
"Daddy"
writes

remembrance
cadaverous
stanzas
scratch
scratch

dunes
valleys
blood-swamp
the-sorrow
twin
moons

bleed
inky
correct
in
red
smiles

# VINCENZO BILOF

## Precipitate Palms

"He said to call him"
Lorraine with the smart
phone. What century

"when you're triggered"

even when she's bound
I like to hear her voice.

"I think you remember something"

threat of violence awakens
truth. Me.

"you can ask for it"

a good man would apologize
for the confusion. tip
his hat. beg forgiveness.
release her.

"but you don't ask, you take"

doesn't believe orchids
touch lips
flowers swallowed by

"turn it on"

jingle and the icon.
black sucks rose floods

# THE HORROR SHOW

toys in a field
girls who can still die
before they die

(there is no more speech for me to surrender,
    birds follow the circuit paths
    charred brain juice
    like the spiderwebbed concrete
    the baked sewage of computer
    porn. Captured with my mouth
    wide open, a passion for
    lights and the power,
    the infinite can be touched,
    browsed,
    splattered on blogs
    or social torture
    chambers where
    we die a million deaths
    to live once, I've been
    in these worlds before,
    my imprint upon the digital
    hell, my eyes are ripped open
    pictures of dead people
    on city streets
    satellite creatures see
    homicide designs
    patterns dropping
    into ancient ruins
    and I can see everything.
    This is how God sees,
    and there is nothing but
    blood where the flowers
    are supposed to be crying.
    I have been here before
    and I might still be imprisoned.
    There's a picture of me
    or a book or two I've written

slices of world melt
and I've lived before.)

"I can show you how to call him"

Power over life and clouds,
fist-cradled. Poets don't
need a universe to slay.
Just innocent lives.
Now the past has a phone number.

"hurt me before you hear his voice"

she knows what I've done before
her life is already over
terminates here
I didn't really believe it until now.

"you'll do worse if you wait, please, for me."

Earth Tones

"You are him."

    "I have learned it."
(Wind scatters the signal)

"We've had this conversation before."

    "I'm not surprised."
(Breathing into sound)

"This time is different. You have a victim."

    "I think . . . I've had others . . . a wife
    and son . . . missing . . . their lives
    are returning to me. Have I
    remembered this much

before?"
(Feel the smirk)

"Something like that. Have you slept? Accidentally?"

"Yes. Once. I remembered things.
This woman, Lorraine. You paid her
to possibly die? There's a good
chance I'll kill her."
(Soft chuckle)

"How does that make you feel?"

"Like I'm going to kill her.
Aren't you supposed to
convince me to . . . let her
live?"
(Sigh)

"That's your question? Rather surprising."

"You're playing a game, aren't you?
With me? With my soul?"
(Sigh)

"Soul? You would've argued there isn't one. Or maybe you don't have one. It's not a matter of playing a game. I promised I would help you. You wanted a cure for *you*. The more you wrote, the more you isolated yourself. The more you isolated yourself, the more you needed me. This is a tiresome conversation. I want to know what happens to Lorraine."

"You don't want to save her.
I don't know why I want
to hear the screams. I see
words in blood, a glow
that can cure hunger."
(HMMMMMM)

"I can do more with your mind than even you can imagine. Your mind is the pathway to a cure . . . a cure the world needs but doesn't know it needs."

    "Because someone is paying you."
(Cough)

"That's part of it. Will you kill her? Maim her? Your wife's face was in different corners of the living room . . . does that repulse you? Will you do the same to Lorraine?"

    "Was I repulsed the last time
    you told me what I did to
    the woman I married?"
(Silence)

"Are you repulsed now? Want to know what happened to Danny?"

    "She's not afraid,
    you know. I mean,
    she looks at me with
    wide eyes, and I can
    see her breathing,
    but she doesn't mind
    dying. You convinced
    her to love me."
(Pause)

"Interesting. We're all just numbers on a data chart, but I can change that. The mind is a wasteland of dust, but inside your mind there is water, the percentile of usage
higher, energy conducted at a speed faster than thought. Within your chemical dump is every malady in the handbook condensed into one meat. Madness incarnate."

    "Impossible."
(Chuckle, grin splits the face)

"If you kill Lorraine and receive the past, then my methods will prove successful . . . then we move on to my second phase."

"I won't kill her."

(Sigh)

"To spite me. But that won't work. Because you're going to kill her, and it's not your choice to make."

("I didn't ask him why I killed anyone, or why I can't be found).

**VINCENZO BILOF**

# Loading the Years

    Who can remember
wind or genocide
frozen fingers clutching headlines
nine-minute horror stories
    Catalogued into:
electrons, melting American

cheese radioactive style.
    A stay-at-home mother
and her son, they mystery.

    Lindbergs, Ramseys,
(upon which Raven did Earhart fly)
screams pasted onto seconds
echo in the wishing well.

    The faces fade into code,
binary mouths asking
where Daddy has gone. Nobody
else can mourn the memory
    trapped in search engines

firing into breathable air,
water to drown their eyes.

# CHAPTER SIX
## Visitation with the Ghosts

## Intestinal

Hammered screams into dry wall
splashes of our lives
canvas painted homicide

Stranded in blank screens
calling you, your name
calling you, come to me
be with me
see me
need me
hear me
marry me again and again

clawing at the stubble
reaching for your eyes
my tongue rolls the name
betrayal-flayed
prisoners bound with rings

These pictures dressed in red
smiles bleeding the future
shall I slay myself again in white?
shall I stand before ovens
and count the shades of flame?

Sleeping upon dinner plates
you've forgotten our child's name
sleeping on sidewalks,
slumping over lawn mowers
waving at the neighbours with pride
he's not an invalid, I said.
Everything's okay in our home.

# Cutter

(Palms against the ears

        fists hold the eyes)

                                held

"Leave me"

(The echo of words portrayed
         *tap tap tap tap tap tap tap*
almost complete
this verse)

Languages sighed at once the question
"I                 am                 making
    dinner"

No I don't remember that dress

    (turkey holiday

    was I there for that?)

"Do you want this leg?"

*Oh my God stop please it hurts please it hurts please oh God*
    Give thanks for the feast is good

Isn't she beautiful or the body how wonderful thou art

# THE HORROR SHOW

how wonderful thou art
pretty girl
"Aren't you hungry?"                  Not thankful after all, it seems

I can see a face in stainless steel
you handsome devil (

                              exclaimed the edge
                              prayer for a napkin to
soak

                                        pirouettes like
sweat
) we can be thankful together.

**VINCENZO BILOF**

# Remembering that Day

Die sections full with playtime daydreams
thread the needle, pretender without screams.
My murdered way forgave the concept of lungs
slipping through red puddles instead of giving hugs.

Body-paint-swimmer licking the fingers of family
how they loved, how they adored until finall
paintbrush coloring wife on the drapes
redecorate with the urge of endangered primates.

*Aaaaahhh,* belching with fingers in my mouth
a meal fit for a king cooked in my house.
Steam rises from the pan;
hunter-gatherers murder when they can.

All I wanted for dinner was an expensive liver
you disappointed because you were never a giver;
your fists shaking my heartbeat with every demand,
no wonder I fell asleep without conscious command.

Twirling through mirrors with a new hairpiece
these are not extremes but a way to find peace.
Now I remember that I was a poet;
intestines slathered over shoulders; that's how you do it.

"Hello doctor I don't recognize you,
pardon the mess I've been in quite the mood
I won't mind chains, for I've seen paradise
the universe is composed of blood and lice."

# THE HORROR SHOW

I don't know this music or recognize this mess
my editor can read the blood in her dress.
I'm prepared for rejection even though it's my opus;
dedicated to the masses because this is their focus.

I remember I used a new sledgehammer
your skull looked pretty when it was battered.
Look at me ghost, wraith, spirit, corpse,
I gave you all my money and this was par for the course.

Danny was still alive when your eyes rolled to Hell
he watched vertebrate get ripped out of your shell.
Before I showed him a pair of scissors
I told him how you aborted his sisters.

Maybe he knew what was wrong with me;
Wiser than gods who give nothing for free.
There's my name on another blank check,
Paid for you fantasy before opening your neck.

VINCENZO BILOF

## Love's Tattered Phase

This is where you
beg
for my forgiveness
down on your knees
peer through this veil
no Hell save
what I can deliver

I promised I would never leave you

Here I define
concepts of marriage
sharing of blood
liquids of disease
dying for love

passages and atriums
the siren wails
labyrinthine timidity
fingers frozen by years

tell me about curing the moon

what these bones have wrought
dust for dirges
phantasmal solace
where the sun hides

Don't forget rotting soul
you will burn
in the glacier

# THE HORROR SHOW

reflections the prismatic
versions of my mistakes
searing, melting away

through the veil.

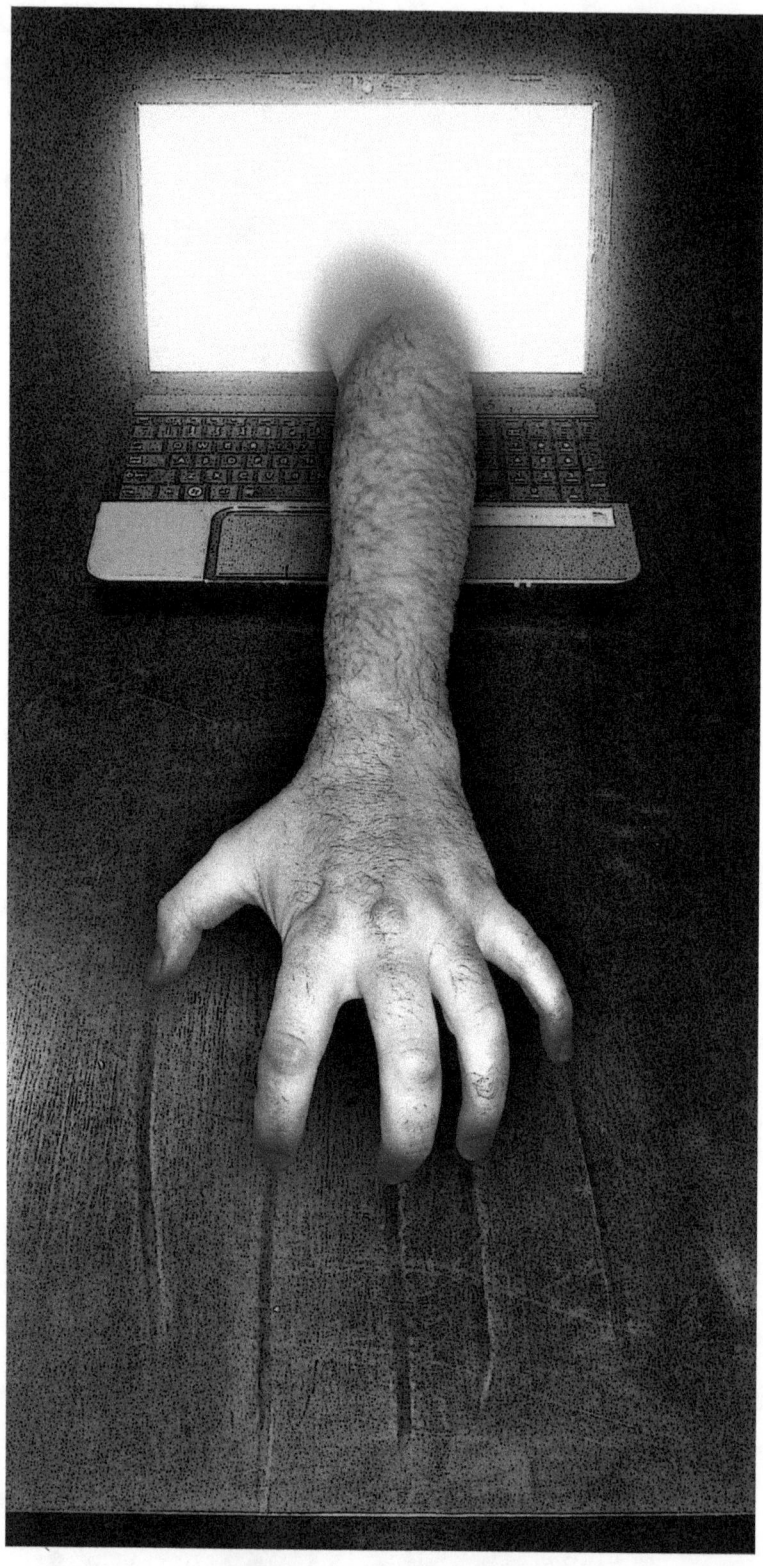

THE HORROR SHOW

## Watching the Sun Burn

Dad, we sat upon the cliff together and you held my hand,
you pointed at the sunrise and said,
    "That's the sun, and someday
    it will die."

I need to whisper now.

I could feel you beside me, your strength
like guitar strings
    slowly plucked
kind of like the one I owned.

Maybe you've seen it. Mom said you bought it.
An acoustic, leaning against a bookshelf
and I have your last book facing out
    you can see it, with your signature
    inside.

We were at a convention again
I walked up to the table with the book
and you signed it, with these big dark sunglasses
    some people in suits behind you,

the doctor

too, but I think he's a friend now. I said
hi, you smiled and signed the book.

When we got home
you (Mom always said you were at work)
disappeared

# VINCENZO BILOF

for three days
I brought you food one night. You were sitting
       in a
computer, I mean in front of it. I thought maybe you saw me.

I pointed at the clouds, and you smiled a little
even if they weren't really clouds at all.
Maybe you were going to say something else.
(I don't know, but I wish I did)

The sky was red like Kool-Aid. There was
a thought in my head         about cigarettes
I was sure you would say
a word, and maybe I could ask if you
would listen to me play the guitar, but
I don't know if I did.

Could music make the sun die,
maybe I thought, or wanted to
but it's there now.

There were two of me, I think one
at my first funeral.
       (Grandma was a nice lady whenever I saw her, but I don't know

if I ever did see her just a thought about eyes and lipstick

an impression I had, a moment somewhere,

that's all. And she was in her casket but you
disappeared. I almost thought you were
home in the computer again
making another thing,

Mom had a black veil over her
                                face and someone said it wasn't
because of Grandma,

# THE HORROR SHOW

and I looked and found you

sleeping

in a chair, but I was afraid you weren't alive. I wanted to wake you but I couldn't.

I stood there, trying to see if you were still breathing. Your fist was on your cheek. I remember the gold buttons on your suit because Mom said you looked like an idiot monk and I felt the need to say something,

maybe tell you
        there was a man by the casket
        wondering if he could get an autograph.

You were sleeping but someone was dead and it wasn't you. I forgot it was Grandma and I waited. I knew I shouldn't be around when you woke up. You taught me that once. Mom taught me that several times. "Don't come near when he sleeps." *I remember.*

Your eyes opened
a punishment I needed from you
when you asked who I was
if I was real
a shiver instead of tears,
I realized you were actually dead
the whole time)

In the quiet I could feel
a conversation:

        could an apology make
        the skeleton dance

words that make me think of poems
or music from my fingers,
the ones you created with the flesh of your own,
skinned by keys with letters on them;

    rocks and stone against meat
    hanging from a cold ceiling.

This is why sunlight doesn't hurt anymore.
Your hand was there, but

I'm the only one who remembers
because it didn't happen.

*(why doesn't Constantia sleep anymore? Lorraine might have a picture of herself as a baby inside her purse. Constantia wanted me to love her forever, until the cliché passed us by. Danny, Doctor Humphrey, Mother, alleys, bitterness, birds trapped inside of bricks. a resurrection of green roses and blue rabbits, furry ones, dripping in the vomit of men who sleep where the moon hides)*

# CHAPTER SEVEN

## Interview with the Witnesses, Character and Otherwise

## THE HORROR SHOW

# Evening News

One our country's greatest mysteries
might be solved.

A man who bears a striking resemblance to

a poet who's been missing since (    )

may be prowling the streets of downtown Detroit.
While authorities have denied the rumors that
investigators have covered up the murder
of his wife, aged (        )

and his (        )
-year-old boy,

who're also missing, suggest there's no evidence the poet
has been seen in the city where he grew up.

"Well, to this date the case remains open."

FLICKERING BETWEEN LINES

" . . . he would read to his son every night. Hard to believe"

"nobody saw him for years after his fourth book"

"From poverty, a man who
         REPRESENTS THE AMERICAN DREAM"

(artists behind coffee tables damage their hands
fish swimming behind glass faces

java masters pointing at a madman's words)

" . . . Despite reports to the contrary, we have not questioned any potential witnesses . . . "

the shadow man remains a mystery
bleeding beneath the moon.
"That's like saying a man can kill love."

## THE HORROR SHOW

# Look at this Poem

he said it was his first.
I remember laughing and saying,

you know, uh,

I'll keep it and maybe
I can sell it for a million bucks
someday.

He was pretty, long eyelashes
and he was always laughing
at something only he could hear.

Everyone knew
who he was.

Came up to me after Spanish
and said, "Hey."
Never talked to him.
I opened the paper

he said, "I hate poetry
but I figure I would
give this to you
because you wrote it,
not me."

> *Let's watch this knife together*
> *bleed and cry in thunderstorm weather*
> *sleeping beneath trees with dark sunglasses*
> *counting the sequins on your bra*

*before tomorrow's classes*
*I can taste your face and eat your*
*tears,*
*Nobody else likes you because*
*you don't have your tongue pierced*
*rumors in the dark you know*
*you can be like the wind and start to blow*
*against the side of your mouth*
*until you start to cry*
*feel your throat pulse against my*
*inner thigh*
*scream when I'm ready into both of my ears*
*be happy I'll remember you*
*for the rest of my years.*

Nobody liked me before,
I mean I thought I was pretty
in my black phase,

it was nice to see him outside my window
one night. I undressed for him.

We did that for a few nights.
    My parents were gone
        once.

He had a knife, cold
I remember how cold.

"Kids our age think about dying
all the time.
Would you scream for me? Please?"

Nobody ever believed me, you know.
I still have the scars,
the first time I saw so much blood,
the knife between my legs, cold.
He made life

# THE HORROR SHOW

beautiful, for the first time.
I think our time's up.

Back to my cell.

## Suffering with Strangers
## (Excerpt from Interview, 2003)

Of course I loved him
what kind of question
is that?

Doctor, this is confidential?
He doesn't know
about the file.

I know it wasn't autism,
or maybe they

weren't sure. Or I wasn't.
Couldn't understand.

Needed loud noises
to fall asleep.

Wasn't afraid of much
until he was a boy,

I remember a thunderstorm.
Wasn't on drugs before

I had 'em. Answered that before.
Just marijuana.

Doesn't count.
Everybody loved him.

# THE HORROR SHOW

He would put my words
into patterns. Did that

to his Grandpa, too.
Convinced mathematics

was a language from
outer space. HA HA HA!

Music had to be ear-splitting,
I would mumble

for several minutes,
he'd sleep but fitfully.

He was happy in school,
though. Except when

he did his thing with ants.
Whenever they gathered

thousands of them, swept
them into a bowl.

He liked to smash them,
said he wondered why

they were silent
when they died,

thousands of them
millions, silent.

## VINCENZO BILOF

# Lover at the End of Time

You can say I've admired his work or maybe you can
even say I've dreamt of him maybe
even fantasized about him. No
I mean I've wondered what he
might look like behind all

those words he like wears a mask
at least that's what I feel anyway
and besides, what else is there to
consider, I wonder yes, what else
could there be? I think you have

to be a part-time masochist and a
full-time narcissist all at once to be
a writer. Who else is seeking a greater
confessional, or adventure, or
something profound, the purveyors of
rhetorical questions and cold war spy
thrillers, you know the type
the ones at the grocery store.
I don't go for the romances

because I have his words. His words
fill me but I always had the sense
that his writing had more to do
with nightmares or worlds he visited
in nightmares . . . ? He reached down
and found the primal
and I was afraid to read
the next poem because
I didn't know that

murder could be
painted in
beautiful

words

like blood
as one massive
thick stroke of red
paint across a canvas.
Smart for a stripper, eh?
Yeah I've thought about it,
I mean I thought about it you
know, I thought I found a kindred
spirit in his words he was pretty cool
got me through high school and I thought
my body was something I owned and it had
the only thing that could get people to survive

my presence because I was beautiful and intelligent

and that makes me dangerous

but look what they've done to me? I'm not that smart, you know. But I like to read poetry. Do you like poetry? Listen, I understand. Yes, he did pay me.

But I wouldn't let him pay again. I'd give him every piece of my flesh if he so desired to scrape it off with a knife. Maybe he'd be kind enough to let me watch him do it. Yes. Watch him do it.

**VINCENZO BILOF**

# The Starch Monsters

sEEmed normal What do I knoW?

A goOD student, did
                               all his work

Laughed, got along. sEEmed well
adjusted.

HATed poetry. Wondered aloud
                               why study these alcoholics
                               drunks
                               suicidal, melodrama queens

Had to read his file
he stank because he was living
on the street by choice.

So I was in the building late one day
he came by the room and said
there was something. We rarely
                               talked.

HallWAYS were empty.
Inside a bathroom stall
where everything was white,
he pointed to a skeleton.
A rat skeleton.

       He

# THE HORROR SHOW

Found it drowned
after a thunderstorm

several weeks ago.
Placed it in the vent of boys'

    room.

Nobody EVer noticed.
I couldn't move.

    Imagine how I stood
    like I was being choked
    I mean I couldn't
    breathe. The first
    thought in my head

was I to blame for
what might happen
next?

Because there was a long silence.
                        Extending. Endless.

His eyes looKED
black. Wide and black. Like

the thing he killed.

"I wanted to show you
what poetry looks like."

I never told anyone
because I wanted
to forget.

Quietly, I've been
                      the anonymous

boring man since then,
and this isn't about me,

>	but I never did my job
>	and let him disappear
>	into MANhood

because I was too afraid
of the truth.

# THE HORROR SHOW

## Street Testament

This is what goes for art 'round here
Fire in a can, carts full of gold
mouths full of blood
dust full of chalk
Half my brothers faded into the brick
you can see their names scribbled there
Wrecking balls kill Shakespeare
ALL TIME IS HOLLOW
      That one is his
Eyes sticking to the wall
      a kid lived here once
      we've seen his face
      glued to glass
He mentioned a woman drowning
      in her own blood
there was a game show on TV, he described it
      a woman jumping up and down with her eyes wide and full of
      tears
      her hands clapping together magnetized
      she was cured like a leper
      her face recorded like a saint traced in crayon
woman in her blood reached up
some fingers went missing
glass wouldn't break today
death isn't silent it happens
everyone watches from windows
REMOTES IN THEIR HANDS
      that one is his, too
he told us we were heroes
When he returned he'd already disappeared
into bookshelves

## VINCENZO BILOF

this is where he played and sang
we're the lepers under ice
      he is the torch
burnt by stars.

# Razor Blurred

In space,
a teenage runaway
he promised he wasn't
a hippie. It was on
his mind.

Now a bunch of us cats
was huddled round
a fire. Cold as hell,
know whut
um saying?

The money smells nice
so yeah, maybe I
remember what he needed.
Said his mother was

an epidemic
of pain. Wiped her tears
across his brain
to scar his skeleton.

He was on bad
shit, like his eyes
disappeared, all this
talking about poetry,
a dream splashing
through a hurricane

and acid, maybe.
Face looked like a rubber

mask. Said we only know
nothing until we know
how to feel blood on our hands.

Now, I'm feeling like I
gotta push him through the brick.
Wanted to show us
something he had
in the trunk of Mommy's car.

I remember what he said:
"I wrote down everything
she said before I chopped
her up. We had a good
conversation about storms
and shopping malls. Met her
at the frozen slushee machine.
Told her I had
the best trip she could take.

Well, I know she's pretty.
Her words were even nicer.
Wrote poems between
screams. You know
what it's like out here
in these alleys; loneliness,
an abyss. Where fear
is afraid to tread."

He stuck around
for a few months
after that.

# THE HORROR SHOW

## Lorraine

The colonel dropped the file on the doctor's desk.
Another day.

Imagine soldiers immune
to the emotional
effects of war.
Imagine a world without
madness.

The perfect candidate, Doctor.
I
think
you'll
agree.

The narrative of a madwoman.
She played with fire.

Recreate the episode,
Doctor.
Imagine
her
doing it.

(I already know who she is. I've watched her.)

Behind the dumpster, Lorraine hefts the trash bag,
drops it in.

A man slams her against the wall.
He hand clamped around her jaw.

# VINCENZO BILOF

Her eyes

don't move. A cat

poised.

No words.
Un
zip.

She's down on her knees,
head working, back and forth
back
and forth.

Now her eyes move.
They
open.

Stars might be exploding.
Head stops.

He slips away and
shudders against
the opposite

wall.

Her lips are wet,
in the glow of light from across the street,
through the narrow aperture of brick.

Shuddering,

he falls into the black world
from when he
shall not remember himself
or this event

but
he
will
know
her
lips

when he sees her again.

"I'll be here for you," she whispered.
It wasn't the first time, nor the last.

After the image closes,
"Colonel,
she wants
to
make
him
happy.
She'll do anything."

# He Took Me to a Ballgame

Today, I turned eight years old, and I had such a great time!
Dad came out of his room because he remembered my birthday.
He didn't last year. He's always busy
with his job and it gets tough for him because his eyes are getting
bad so he has to wear the sunglasses but that's
okay. Mom doesn't know but I like it when he wakes me up to
show me some of the poems. He reads to me but he also reads
*my* poems and I like that. The baseball game was a lot of fun
only Mom didn't know about it and we knew she would be mad.
Dad was smiling and laughing like I remember him but when we
were at the game he remembered he had to do something
and he stared at the big screen that sits above the field. He kept
staring at it and he said
the crowd was beautiful because
it was so loud. He didn't move and I had to go to the
bathroom. I thought he fell asleep and I can't remember the
game because I was scared he wouldn't be able to move again. Mom
bought me the game I wanted and I played it all night.

## CONNIE

This is my attempt
you muther
remember my dreams why don't you
scribbling on a cheap coffee

shop napkin.
You swagger over and
       "I'm sorry I came in here
       because I wanted to see
       what a poet looked like
       and I'm glad I found one.
       Christ wept, you're a
       madman's bad daydream."

Eighteen years without
a word
fingers shake
while you melt in front of the computer

into a puddle of porn

gave you the son you wanted
gave you eighteen years
so I could sit on the doctor's lap
and play
while you win millions
with the poems I wrote
to save our souls

eighteen fucking
eighteen can you believe

# VINCENZO BILOF

I died so you could live
yeah that's right
your friend the doctor
partner in crime
sex toy god of my flesh

I wrote the poem about the killer
look at me now
the invisible woman

# VINCENZO BILOF

## Parks in Reverse

um so
his face was on
the glass
loved the octopus
something about
liquid tentacles
or fluidity,
he told me later

when I held him
close with the storm
creeping, he shivered
and said he remembered
the octopus
and its silence
its presence and its
reach into
darkness

over mountains and valleys
over oceans and countries
over snow and graveyards
the octopus watches
uncoils

what he said, I remember,
while shaking.

# Fractional Semi-Fiction

Sipping on cold coffee,
a morning, pale,
nothing,

"Excuse me? Is it . . . ?"

Tiny
girl,
sunburnt, stomach
with the little jewel
pierced,

her top covering almost
nothing,
she could be twelve
or forty

freckles, dusty eyes,
alive.

"You'd never
believe,

I'm from Texas,
I love . . . I mean just *love* . . .
your poems . . . I, uh . . ."

she's got his eyes,
hips shift
ripped shorts
legs, red, toes

curling

faces stop, the stomach again
a jewel at the center,

"I have a copy of *Mirrored Eyes,* for
you to . . . sign . . . um, it would be . . . an
honor.

He removed his sunglasses.
His eyes might have
              Been white
              or steel

"Did I write it?"
he asked.

Maybe he was supposed to smile.

Hips shift,
hand in the back pocket,
tip toes, searching
lights,

a book in an arm,
slender, black,
flesh is red everywhere

"You want to be a poet,"

he said.

"Well,"

hanging, he extended his hand
for the book

# THE HORROR SHOW

He stared at the
cover,

"If I sign it, would you
      be willing to
      let me lick
      your stomach
      and then eat
      your eyes?
      Later, in my
      office;
      and then I can
      staple
      your freckles
      to my chest
      and wear them."

Her body quivered.
Hips,

"Oh, I'd love that,
I mean, it would be an honor
to be with you, to hear
your words,
alone. My God, I mean
sorry, don't mean to offend . . . "

"My son won't be home,"
he stared at the cover,
"your name?"

"Tawny . . .
You're my . . . inspiration," she breathed.

"You'll swallow everything
I give you," he said.

# VINCENZO BILOF

She nodded,
the jewel swayed.

The power of poetry.

# CHAPTER EIGHT
# (Fragments, Evidence)

## Echoes from the American Crypt

**THE HORROR SHOW**

From: *Confessions from Post-Apocalyptic Mars*
(Black Swan International Publishing, NY, New York, 1998)

# Foreword

It was described to me what it might be like to lie down in a bed of lava. With your eyes unfocused. Something otherwise dreary. Not a private horror.
This man could draw demons with his fingertips. Crafted them out of your imagination and not his own. A mass-murderer of the sensory.

# VINCENZO BILOF

# Colonies on Fire

We court beneath stars
Neruda's tears
Acid stains on her blouse
Sorceries bloom in lavender gardens
Her knuckles are clad in gold
Promises melt like snowdrifts
under sea. She wants to crawl
into my years where I might
be wandering.

## A Collection of Weddings

Looking for mirrors buried in the king's tomb
Stolen iron princess
Raped like my destiny
        Broken like minutes

Sunrises after midnight
Remember when she was beautiful
I do, sealed
White chambers paint the names
        one wife or three,

We don't have to be afraid
to be alone
hanging gardens full of vines
thorns, prick,
blood runs, staining white
or velvet, or peace.

**VINCENZO BILOF**

From: *Mirrored Eyes* (Black Swan International, NY, New York, 1999)

# Biography of a Lucid Dream

He was a poet. A status tant
amount the
note
worthy pers
onal version of the antiq
uated vi
cissitude of mir
rors, you've seen, I know, a sta
tus otherwise noteworthy
on the shores of Demeter or Phobos.

## Rainbows Jade the Chamber

Ideas massacred upon pages
Why don't we open each other's ankles
Swing from chandeliers or cradle babies

    which
belong to strangers to make up for
lost time?

A beautiful boy who remembers planets
in the alarm-clock glare of tired hours
documents stare up at him
I wanted to save him, once

Let me write in first person a while longer
I don't want you to die anytime
before Christmas.

# VINCENZO BILOF

From: *Crooked Dining Room Pictures*
(Black Swan International Publishing, NY, New York, 2001)

## Hands Cut from Plastic

jagged and cold dead and desolate a laugh worth forgetting. As they
say in the business.
We tracked his alter ego for a number of years.
A murderer of the flesh.

A seducer of women with words whose familial tongue belonged to the
*mad* culture, now deceased these past seventeen-thousand centuries,
a spirit worth wearing to
a party dangling from a necklace,
(let's say, for the sake of argument, this artist killed one or two people,
maybe a woman and a boy)

because you need to hear "where did you get that?" to verify your
loneliness. Your suffering. The poet is
eternal or something like that. A constant martyr
for love and the imagination and nightmares.

My son coughs into a vase
because there are no dogs sleeping
beneath the spiked heels
or Mommy's scowl.
Isn't she lovely?

The hippogriff stares.

## THE HORROR SHOW

# Horses While Chained

jk jk jk
omg u brb
or else I
stained
letters
veins ope on
kybrd

H4u pls
do it sideways
flkring monitor
unplugged
warranty doesn't
cover blood

W/blood on
my thighs
slathered
n slang
fav star
O Mouth
do it on her face this time

Can U C
now carpet wife
lives beyond
doorways
pissed at
accidents, don't crash
let me finish

# VINCENZO BILOF

there's a son
Not allwd 2 lstn
WAEF
hands slppry

mse falls in pool
f red

(my toenails need to be clipped, holy . . . )

the fnsh
she has a smile
dnt crash dnt crash
lmst done
blood rush
let the head
fall
srrder 2 kybrd

scrn out
blck room

UWIWU

I can't wait to see her face when she walks in and sees this mess she will clean up because she's such a faithful wife, yes she is. Forgiveness is the best revenge.

# THE HORROR SHOW

From: *Unfinished Worlds*, published with permission from the Estate of _____
(Black Swan International, NY, New York, 2999)

## The Killer's Catharsis

I like swimming pools. I mean,
they've got all the genes
and the sicknesses and the health
and the ocean
you know, what's so bad
about everybody in one place
or planet? What's so bad
about falling in love with
coagulated flesh

piles and piles melting
butter into hands.

Not sure who killed all
the alleyways, where I
nightmared into flames
with old men and fleas,
lies,
sparrows.

Something misses itself
between the wet
and the coffee shop,
Connie glances up in memoriam
of her destiny from a napkin.

Who's been writing these poems?

# VINCENZO BILOF

When was I awake? I remember
a wedding to a poet, a woman
who said she would never
have to breathe again
if I just whispered into her

ear
the screams.

She's been sleeping with

a doctor, someone I'm
supposed to know.

I don't feel funny,
or sick.
I keep thinking about
a thunderstorm shaking

Connie, and she has
an octopus over her
face, soaked in tentacles,
and I'm in love. Think:

if I kill her slowly enough,
she'll remember why
we married.

There was a moment at our wedding,
yeah, now I can recall.
Her eyes danced for a moment
beside me, lace and shadow,
white on black,
my hands eclipsed her waist,
I saw mirrors behind her face,
her smile was full of sadness
and mourning,

# THE HORROR SHOW

for youth surrendered
and the soldiers wrote letters home
to their mothers, the revolution
ended, flags
buried beneath bodies on a hill.
Mirrors
behind her face,

pools of light
burning darkness at her feet,
slow, liquid octopus hair,
glancing upon,
touching, eyes sliding into
shade,
the smile fails to wither,
remains.

crescent reflections,
cast into visions of
a different world,
together made of our
words, already etched into
our fingers,
my hands slithered
upward,
over,
her throat.

Connie, your heart was
beating so quickly,
your lips parted and
I drank your kiss,
ripping your head backward,
eating breath.

I don't feel funny.
If she's not in the mood to scream
my intentions will save

her soul, or whatever swims
in her blood.

What will Danny think?
He's out there, hiding
from the ghost.

A colossus holds us
in fists made of obsidian,
because murder is the
search for truth
and majesty of art.
Art is predicated

on mortality. Thoughts.

# THE HORROR SHOW

(*We're under the assumption that Constantia snuck into his room while he was at the hospital for one of his extended stays. The following excerpt was recorded onto the poet's computer and discovered by chance, curiosity, and the title*: PLAY WITH ME TONIGHT)

"Why can't you hear me screaming? This . . . poem . . . I was writing this in the coffee shop when you came in. It's framed, sitting on your bookshelf. I dusted the cobwebs because I didn't recognize it. I'm in your room. I'm in a stranger's castle. I think Danny forgets your name sometimes, maybe on purpose. But the poem . . . I don't recognize the hand . . . uh . . . I'm just . . . thinking about the last book I wrote for us . . . you said I would look pretty with a toilet seat strapped to my back . . . but you forgot you said it . . . this poem . . . it's almost in a different language. I want to write by myself again . . . I've cleaned the semen from your keyboard . . . I have more poems for you . . . it was your idea . . . just a game you said . . . ghostwriting . . . bleeding into each other . . . that's what you said it would feel like, but you're bleeding all over me, or I'm bleeding all over you. I'm dead I think, not me, or not the me I knew."

**VINCENZO BILOF**

# Angel Holocaust

A spider stretches its legs over planets in orbit, revolutions wearing pink regalia while officers lay their swords in the mud.

The poet has folded his hands over his stomach and is watching the ceiling remain in stasis. A room full of dark, a Catholic closet of shame and amber, floral patterns and incense. Some doctor.

"Tell me about your newest poem, the one you were working on last time we spoke."

"We spoke several seconds ago and I think, well, there were some words but I remember you asking me if I could recall my last dream or maybe a nightmare, though the context is escaping me at this moment. Sorry."

"You've been asleep for several minutes. Does this moment feel like a dream?"

"A discourse on pornography, like something that is an abstract of physical tension or a release not unlike homicide, a comparison although I wouldn't know the second one and I haven't even been thinking that way you know; I'm not like that, I would never. I love my wife and son even if I forget what they look like for long stretches of road or imagination."

"Your dream?"

"A poem about the machine. Earth boxed into electronic messages broadcast through beams of light and code while I typeaway, and you get tempted while the mind wanders, you can look at, even read anything you want. Change a tire, build a bomb, load a gun, dissect a child, watch people having sex, then you can read headlines that have nothing to do with words or meaning; some pictures thrown in for good measure, the gown is quite fashionable, things like that. You know how it goes. Red carpet treasons. The machine is the mind in a prison because you see all and it knows all; there is so much we can learn but sex is there, you know, all depravities can exist at once along the continuum."

# THE HORROR SHOW

How would anyone grasp the power of the screen and its message, the way it mocks or surrenders? Words appear though fingers refused to speak, and a doctor wants to know about poetry.

"Computers," the doctor mused aloud. "What would life be like without them?"

"Voices muted by the overload. Who can scream the loudest in a vacuum, that's what we all want to know. Maybe read about a cat in a tree or a cancer survivor, the affliction of man, a curse like a program embedded in binary code traced along pages and pages, though I suppose pages themselves are burning in the dust as we speak."

A man can drown in the vomitorium of languages that can hear themselves suffering the misfortunes of fate. Continents colliding and melting into a heartbeat pumping through electrical currents all the way to California or the moon. A pipeline to tomorrow when nobody really needs information, everything is there.

The doctor sighed and tapped his pencil against a clipboard. "I wanted you to tell me about your poetry. I like to hear about your latest projects. Are you still bothered by the Nobel Peace Prize . . . ?"

"I've recited most of it," the poet found the creases over his knuckles to be interesting. "I don't know if poetry exists. My wife . . ."

An invalid looming over a box through which light shines, radiation glare scratching away at the eyes until his wife places a spoon in his mouth. There are other men in the house because he can no longer use the bathroom or tie his shoes without losing his mouth. A married man becomes a ward of the state and Daddy isn't feeling well but he loves us so let's take care of him. Words spoken underwater while the subconscious plays with flame.

Scribbling across a page, a pen perched between fingers.

"We can know everything and we're afraid," the poet reminded him, an echo of words he shared with a woman or a boy, maybe typed into a program; ideas and thoughts "saved" like Descartes can chew gum while arguing with Pythagoras about time and the alphabet.

"How often do you masturbate?"

Who asked that question? Who can answer? Asylums are cold places but the office has all the comforts a prison in the sky can provide. Howls of torment while the brain freezes and a woman comes running into the room. Ripping pages from books and sleeping inside the pile of ideas left behind by dead men, afterimages slipping away, words forever "saved" until deletion. Thoughts given form, ghosts tapping at the window. The poet answered and spoke to several strangers, including a woman who used to serve him coffee at Starbucks, a child-like smile on her face forever. There was also a cat who spoke in Haiku, fingernails upon concrete.

"Rest assured, your wife and son are doing well," the doctor explained to nobody. "They have talked to me about moving you where you can be taken care of more . . . thoroughly. There are some tests we'd like to run. Good doctors from Washington, military doctors, everybody . . . you're very special."

"I want to tell you about a staircase. I'm walking up the staircase and around me there are stars as if I'm in outer space but I can still breathe, or maybe I'm not breathing"

(at all. There're pillars, cracked pillars beside the staircase like Roman columns or Greek I don't know the difference, and this woman like a holy spirit speaks to me but I can't hear the words, and I'm thinking and very conscious of what I'm thinking. I want to know what she's saying but the words aren't meant for me to hear. The woman is floating and there is a window playing with her reddish-brown hair but I can't describe color and how can there be wind in space? I wish that my wife held my hand only her face is somewhat distant or lost like one of the stars, you can touch them or maybe not. I walk up the staircase and there's nothing beneath it and I can see cracks in each step, each step made of stone or glass, some stained glass or marble, porcelain or ice. Nothing is the same and it changes with each passing storm. I'm afraid of falling. Spinning without saying a word but I can't help myself. Through the distant speakers from a real world I've forgotten I can hear politicians debating with each other over stimulus packages that don't stimulate. The exaggerated grunting of women opening themselves up for anything that dares or wants. Music born from a million destinies. Spaceships and soldiers fighting with video game monsters. Highlights from the latest soccer game. The British are coming or they've won. Someone wants to build a bomb but Daddy has said it can't happen today. One world government. Words, letters, and screams)

"there is a box at the top of the staircase. Maybe my wife has left it for me. I'm not supposed to open it. I kneel down and think about praying because it seems proper. A comet explodes or it doesn't. The box is opened like an egg split by a hammer and I'm watching the screen brighten, all knowledge is contained therein and I'm so afraid of it all I just want someone to hear me scream."

# CHAPTER NINE (The Poet)

## Puppet without Limbs

# THE HORROR SHOW

## The Late Show

Another window into the unreal,
the television summons the poet,
touches his face, swirls fingers
through blood pools,
SOMETHING GLANCING.

Stations beamed into the universe
from ideas swimming through
the dark,

satellites.

"Lorraine's always here. The guy
(he comes in and talks to her,
sometimes

he      falls    asleep. Looks

just like that poet guy
(you're asking about)."

Charnel house
surgery on Channel Five
men in masks cut into blood.

Nazis march in shades of gray
to teach lessons.

    (Wet brick and fiery barrels,
    a young man stood and watched
    pieces burn, looking for

prophecy and pain,
amusing thoughts

my mind in its natural state
no drugs here. They didn't
know. Slaughterhouse
to find the sorcery
buried inside)

Coffins before they're purchased.

(I was in a graveyard once.
The perfect date. Name was
Adrian or something like that.
I might be making it up.
A name from a poem maybe,
or a poem about the night
with Adrian.

MEMORIES IMAGINED OR OTHERWISE

Had the dark makeup and
was a bit squirrely. Shoes
slipped in the mud and
rain, you know it had to rain,
now I see it.

She didn't think it was fun
to be pushed into an open
grave. I fell in love
with her for a few moments
because she said a lot
when she screamed.
The feeling is not so hollow
when you recreate it
because it can exist again
maybe).

# THE HORROR SHOW

Explosions and devils chasing fire.

Brick walls and acid-soaked years without acid.

Back to the charnel house. Lorraine refuses to weep.

VINCENZO BILOF

# The Poet's Deliberate Dream: Part 1

Here's something to be forgiven for.
Broadened masquerades, bookended daydreams,
when rainbows become night-terrors. Ice-cream
trucks become carnival attractions and the laughter
of the under-aged mingles with the tears of the hesitant.
Each bloodline guilty of running

through veins, branching roadways, and thunderstorm misgivings.
The pulse of razorburn chanting and
the seconds, miliseconds, stolen years, all multiplied
all manifest, all overreaching. Blooming flowers

of yesterday's summer. You call me a killer? I'm afraid
to know what I wanted to be. I want to burn inside the pages of a book
while it's held in the gnarled figures of a dying old construction
worker. Write this down.

# The Poet's Deliberate Dream: The Sequel

Where do all the dead pens go
        when they're all forgotten and
        (broken thought, image displaced, remembrance,
translucence, misinterpretation)
somewhere, emptied . . . ?

# VINCENZO BILOF

## Boiled Scream

There was a romantic who died
years ago in front of a mountain,
his eyes open while ice
melted over his lips.
In his hands he held a photograph
believed to be a woman,

shapeless, no form worth
mentioning because the lines
faded.

Later, authorities
discovered a love letter
to a nameless woman
in the romantic's home;
he described his dream
of her.

In the description he
mentioned a story
that inspired him,
a tale of woe
about a goddess
who fell in love with
an angel. Both women
met while discussing
the nature of mortal love,
and the goddess wooed
the angel with a story, about

two men who crossed paths
by voyaging between planets;

# THE HORROR SHOW

both defied each other's
perception of form and thought,
but when they met
their curiosity blossomed

and they agreed to explore
each other and
the cosmos.

One of the men was a painter
who designed galaxies,
and they were only men
as gods defined them,
human for the sake of
understanding.
The painter asked his lover
to pose so that he might
compose the universe.

Inside his spiraling wormholes
were two blind children
who held hands
and slept in a tomb
at the edge of time.
They whispered into
each other's ears
while their skulls
joined.

One of the twins
ripped out its eyes
and explained one of them
was made of emerald, the other,
sapphire. Handcrafted eyes
made a saint and a sinner,
sexless creatures dwelling
inside of an abyss
or a labyrinth.

# VINCENZO BILOF

The sinner died over
the fire, and the saint
bled upon each gem. None
of it was painful, for
the sinner and the saint
were romantically in love
with the idea of their world.

# THE HORROR SHOW

## Murder Mongrel

"Describe it to me," Saint Lorraine said.
"Why?"

"I want to anticipate the pain. I want to think I know what it might feel like."
"Why?"

"I don't know what pain is. I've carried the weight of the homeless, the suffering, the mad, on my shoulders. I've carried the world's dumpster atop my head like an Egyptian woman carrying a woven basket full of snakes through a bazaar."
"Why?"

"I toured a sanitarium. I heard the screams of the lonely. I listened to the obsession, the singing, the confusion. I watched invalids drool and women finger themselves behind bars while thinking nobody can see them."

"The first cut. I want you to feel it. It was my intention all along."

"I've been swimming in the piss of the world. You'll remember everything. Homicide will bring you back from the dead."

"You're a martyr."

"No. I'm in love. I'm in love with the damn human race. Don't you see? Everyone's in pain, and everyone's lonely. We're all hiding behind computer screens and paper marriages, when all we want is truth and freedom from ourselves. We're all mad. We're all insane. You can cure them."

"I'll have my memories back when I kill you. When I see your blood. When I splash it across my face. This proves . . ."

"Murder is intimate. It's special."
>"You're worse than I am. I don't know everything about myself, and you know
everything about yourself."

"I want to feel you take me away. I want to see you live again."
>"I think it will hurt. Maybe for a long time. I hope."

" . . . "

" . . . "
"I think I might forget your name."

# The Poet's Deliberate Dream
# Part Three: Untitled

Murder isn't a desperate cry for help, I promise. My biggest concern is the formatting. When sunset and dawn are exactly twelve hours apart. Wrote a poem once about a cigarette burning a hole through my skull, thought it wasn't my skull. Pretend that you're me, come on, pretend that you're me for one moment, and that just means forget everything and just become yourself, I mean forget who you are and become yourself, if that makes sense. The doctors wanted to see if I could kill and be reborn. Therapy involves sacrifice and sacrifice requires pride and pride requires greed and greed requires that you wake up and waking up requires that you stop dreaming and to stop dreaming you must begin sleeping and to begin sleeping you must wear yourself down and to wear yourself down you must experience the abyss of debt. They said that I was married, that I loved her. I don't know how to do this.

# Jester Pyre

I used to turn on

        lawn        mowers        just        to
        hear

the noise. Worms in a blender

still didn't

        scream.

Poured a mouthful
    of broken bones

into Constantia's cereal.

        don't        "call me Connie." Beautiful wife
                              of *mind*.

Sunflowers on Christmas
    blame Danny for
        fire

Went for a walk
    (she was surprised and called
        the        doctor.)

used a brick
    Constantia wasn't pleased
    blood makes her squeamish
    so does clumped hair.

sticking    to    it.

## Junkyard Plain

"Your hair is pretty;
now I remember
hurting you while half-asleep.
Semen spilling onto garbage

      I could never hurt you
      so falling asleep was easier
      for both hemispheres.

Seconds return, glimpses,
sullen phrases and arguments
sliding over

shoulders, a computer screen

said it might be God
speaking.

Oh, my, now I REMEMBER! Everything
that can be known or unknown,
modified or damaged, exists

      in words.
I knew I liked poetry

when I put a frog
into my mouth to hear its
noise inside my skull. Searching

for
echoes.

# VINCENZO BILOF

Mother said the frog
wouldn't feel
a thing after
tomorrow. Couldn't waste the blood.

Words, languages, monkeys eating
mirrors while laughing

build the machines

words the product of sorcery
or thought-murder.

Your eyes are pretty
but they're not too loud."

# THE HORROR SHOW

## Verona, Where We Lay

Every poem was a suicide
letter
the woman listened to me
rescued me
brought me back

I like when she gags
on the toothbrush, eyes
full of tears, wide
pleading,
_____won't speak

terminating letters at the end of a love song

"what happens at your funeral?
    I'm not judging you
    but you're not afraid
    to feel this,
    my love."

New car smell,
or baseball cards,
or mulch,
sensation and courtship
when sex feels like
an event during a revolution
a moment of martyrdom for the species
an event during a revolution

"what happens at your funeral?"
    I'm not afraid to

visit or remember you,
the highest love
is this: when a man
is this: when a woman
is this: when Troy
was salted and Aeneas
tripped over a rainbow,
obsession replaces compassion
replaces flesh
love is suicide of the self."

The borders of my eyes expand,
fingertips trace tooth-edges,
like gently petting a dinosaur
or a vagina that hasn't
eaten in years,
there is mercy at
;;;;;;;;;;;;;
the octopus veins twitch.

# CHAPTER TEN
# (The Poet and the Victim)

## Asleep at a Funeral

## Memento of Truth

You can die this way, cry this way,
hide this day, burn this
fate.
Nobody has to unravel the mystery
behind my eyes, the natural
and super-mystical way I carve
into your thighs.
Slightly,
(one gash)
a sordid, artistically-placed
em-dash.
Is that a tear I see fall
from those bright white orbs?

(Can't you see)

this is the work of a poet
and not a millionaire straight from the pages of Forbes?

I'm not some benign social experiment, as you say.
Look at me now because I do this
in a sick and twisted way.
Bleed upon this blade's edge!
Watch as I hover upon sanity's ledge.
Everything you say is another
carefully-concocted lie,
You're like all the others, I think––
stealing another moment of life
before you die.

Why didn't you feel this way before?

# VINCENZO BILOF

# Moments of You

Call me a whore, then.
I've seen this rage before.
"You're just like all the others."
So, can we call this an intimate moment?
Justify your inhumanity:
      (tell yourself it's not real
      it's all my fault, isn't it?)

Maybe you can blame the world
      (so watch it spin, or watch it burn
      watch it churn or watch it carom
      off the skull of some benevolent shithead who
      plays dice or chess or maybe poker with the universe)

This pain is nothing new.
You've hurt me before, just not with the face
you wear now.

You:
A world-famous poet, a suffering malcontent
drenched in your melancholia,
your megalomania.
      Drowning in an ocean of You.

I'm your biggest fan.
I loved your way with words.

Smile.
You were married once. You had a lovely child.
Someone pitied you.
Bouts of narcolepsy complimented by pages

ravaged by your pen.
You killed them both.

Somebody knew you. Studied you. Wanted you.
They injected you.
Tested you.

Here you are.
You think it was all an accident.
But I'm your biggest fan.

Murder isn't an accident.

I was supposed to be saved, but not by them.
By you.

All that darkness swirling within you.
The moon shines through the blinds.
The truth burns a jagged scar across your soul, you—

—who are you.
Believeth in me.
Breathe me.
Do what you want with me.
No mortal man can satiate your lust for blood and pain.
They gave you a codename.

Want to know what it is?

# VINCENZO BILOF

## Words on a Bridge

If I say your name
will you write about me?
The only man I loved
taught me how to die.
And for what.

You can't see love
and you can't see God,
but I have been
searching for clues,
and you showed me
what pain is.

Nobody will know me.
I'll fade, disappear.
The soup kitchen will
feed the insane,
where I found you.

The blade has my face.
I knew I was pretty,
       but you won't see tears.
When I die
they'll have the answers,
finally, a sequence
of fear and memory.

We can see Love
after I die, because madmen
can be cured
of horror. If Love returns . . .

# THE HORROR SHOW

I could be overwhelmed
by the power of this place.

**VINCENZO BILOF**

## Sonnet X

What else is there to say when you witness
the end of a dream?
I can love you forever, you know.
How many times do you live
when you're about to die?

I tilt my head and ponder.
(Whispering now, every so gently, the words like water pouring slowly
into a plastic cup that can burn in a funeral pyre or in some
anonymous incinerator which stands at the edge of the world).

"Tell me what you see.
Do you know what it all means?
The muse of centuries,
the messenger who carried dire tidings
upon winged feed to brave heroes who desperately
clamored for home.
That's how I perceive you.
Love,
speak to me in a designed language,
the fire that rages or burns low
the glowing embers or the skyward apocalypse
that's, you know, what I need.
Your vision.
Tell me.
Yes, that's right, hold my hand.
Everyone was so disappointed
when I told them I wrote stories
about monsters and undead
cannibals. They thought I was Herman MELVILLE!
AND I LAUGHED!

## THE HORROR SHOW

Witness the giant.
He knows for whom the bell burns."

No interest in the benign.
No longer worth it, really.
Nobody can see what she sees.
Nothing can last as long as death.
Nowhere is there a glamorous sense of immortality.
Nonsense, all of it.
No man can ever really die,

Not here,

Not now.
Notice the tears that border the edges of
Nocturne musings, everything
Noted as conclusive,
Nothing.

At last.
Tilt the head.
Breathe.
The chest rises, and then . . .
Collapses, erodes, fades, dies, stops, ceases, ends, dies, burns, cries, sighs . . .

## Sequels Collide

"How do you feel now?"
    "She's pretty, I think.
    That's what you wanted.
    I remember being ripped
    through bright screens."

"You spent a lot of time on the computer."
    "Are you coming for me now?"

"Tell me how you feel."
    "This again. Maybe I should
    tell you what I see. What I
    hear. Spoons falling
    while soup is sucked
    through straws. Flies
    magnified, roam over
    dusty shoulder
    blades. "

"You're writing."
    "Is there a father
    in this blood? Mine or
    hers, I don't know.
    Two of her fingers are
    like towers,
    kind of standing
    upright
    in a fruit bowl."

"I'm listening."
    "Well. Okay. Um.

# THE HORROR SHOW

      This might be her
      forearm. I
      put it on top of the
      the ceiling fan
      and turned it on
      and now everything
      has color."

"Do you know you're going to save the world?"

      "Is that what you want, or
      someone else?"
"Of course there's something for me. You're not the only poet. There's

an art to being a doctor, I think. I understand both creation and deconstruction. Ends and unravelings."
      "Do you think I should
      eat her brain? Did I do
      it before?"

"You don't remember everything."
      "Lorraine wanted
      to love me forever.
      She didn't ask to be
      released. She thought
      I was saving her, not
      killing her, because
      all she could do was save
      others. I, the ultimate
      wretch."

"What were her last words."
      "I'm still looking for them."

"Your need was reawakened when she gave it to you. She sacrificed herself because
she knew I could cure the world with your mind. I needed you to

succumb again. To wake up and remember. To become what you were, to become both the poet and the killer."
"She told me to keep her alive
through as much of it
as I could. She wanted
to watch herself die."

"Does that . . . amuse you?"
"No. It inspires me."

"What do you want to do next?"
"Play in her blood
for a bit, I think."

"After."
"Take a shower."

# CHAPTER ELEVEN (The Poet)

## Afterbirth

THE HORROR SHOW

## Allusion to a Brief Candle

I woke up and wanted to see the master plan
every available nightmare is recalled
My lips open slightly
air
escapes
the knowledge of death becomes awesome
for one moment stand outside and watch yourself writhe in a chair
he is standing over you maybe holding a knife
and
or himself.

Rain comes out of my face
betrayed by a hot sun evaporate
magic all pain ends all tears all that precious
all eaten by heat
to melt flesh becomes hot not cold

the knowledge of death becomes awesome
I have done so many things
I like to think
I have.

**VINCENZO BILOF**

# Speaking through the Moon

Now I know my eh bee sees

    next time won't you kill with me

Twinkle twinkle little knife
    how I wonder how you cut
    in my hands so tightly held
    like a butcher whose been felled
Twinkle twinkle little knife
    now you know that I'm not mad

Slice slice slice her up
    slowly by her ears
    bloodily bloodily bloodily bloodily
    murder causes screams.

**THE HORROR SHOW**

# The Gods and their Action Figure

This is me or someone else
can't I be this version of another man
I've seen on television sculptured
simulacrum

yes. doctor here we are I did it
ding dong me I'm here
not a stranger

I remember                                             *hide the*
*stains*

me I know I am here now I see
we all secretly like to die
I'll go quietly like last time
        *Frankenstein pieced together by*
                *a woman's pen*

that's not my blood only gargoyles
know me or who I am to pretend
how many others or does it matter
more people knew me than I knew
myself I see, in the mirror me

wife and child
                                      *was I*

*there at birth*
not everything is recalled

but here I am who
the man or the image of

# VINCENZO BILOF

hereafter known, title, corpuscular

I don't work like I want you to want
see I kill, see I am, me today

Morpheus has thrown the dice again
these chains have not been mine.

**THE HORROR SHOW**

# Pretty Pictures

Macaroni: You can glue the curved pieces
and design a puzzle,
like this arm. It looks like rubber,
inside you'll find bone.
Uh . . .
Hmm . . .
So what if I . . . ?

Her fingers are soft, she can still tease my hair with delight
or eyes. Okay. So.
On my knees, lean forward, lap it up
and taste. Connie, Danny, my mother, the alleys,
my teachers, my pets,
rats in bathrooms,
an octopus drowning in a thunderstorm.
Doctor Humphrey.
They've returned from the dead.
I can see them all, and this is what Lorraine's taste

delivers. Outside, a car revs its engine,
an ambulance murders silence with a scream,
there's an argument somewhere, a man
and a child.

Hair looks like a spider on the arm
of the chair. Looking at me, just . . .
staring. Maybe you can tell me, fair oracle,
if these eyes belong to her father, or her mother?
It's not important, but how about
this slice of kidney? Still wet . . .
it's not that gross. Don't be shy.
Have some.

# VINCENZO BILOF

## (Words Left on Her Pillow)

The day has nearly ended for you; a grand party held in your honor.

Reserve one moment in your busy day
at twilight
for a cool distraction, a walk in
tall grass to a common pond you've seen

with sideways glances,
and stop. Remove your shoes, stand barefoot
in the cool grass, upon the moist Earth
between your toes.

You've withered with age, your gray hair still streaked with
flecks of the old black,

tracing back youth. You've passed by
this shimmering body
of water before. Your presence is required at the party,
but still you stop, compelled to stare

with your chin tilted upward. Reach around to hold
and clutch yourself against the cold wind as the orange sky
burns away like all those memories you thought lost,

slender fingers of cloud scattered and trailing into
obscure, guessed-at faces with lips that whisper
forgotten names, speaking of forgotten days.

Sit down upon a rock that has been put down upon that shore
for you, as the wind blows coldly; your eyes moisten and the
water seems clear, my love, upon this day

you will recall us. It is an ancient tale
told at fires in low voices, or in the dark

with regret, or in prayer to the unseen.
You'll recall us on that day that has nearly ended,
a moment for you

in your age to see that you have never been alone,
because I have loved you since the beginning of time,
and all time afterward.

# VINCENZO BILOF

## Colorful Birds

Why are they wearing gas masks? I mean, fuck, how many
commandos with guns does it take to arrest a psychotic poet? What is
a poet, anyway?
Is it a collection             of sand or does it move
                                          beside the hands of a clock?

Seven of them. Hands behind their backs.
Parade rest.

It feels like they're staring at me, but that's weird,
because there's so much blood, I mean,
fuck.

Decontaminate me, shut this disease down.
They could have saved Lorraine's life,
but they wanted to make sure

she needed to be dead before they could bring me in.
Now it makes sense.
The doctor wants to cure these people

before they land on Mars or replicate
in Chinese landfills.

Their rubber suits don't have a color.

# VINCENZO BILOF

## No More Monkeys

What you see:

    Millions of dollars or maybe a soul
    Half an arm lying on the television
    Fabrics you'll need to burn
    Hide me
    This is you for years
    Tell me I should be thankful, an urban myth
    designed by hundreds
    of strange mouths.
I suppose you have nothing to say.
    Results and worlds,
    bar graphs in blue and red
    vacations on islands
    full of nymphs
    tropical girls with goddess
    skin smiling, tossing
    hair and clipping
    crusted yellow toenails.

What I see:

    Glasses with a red glare
    your masterpiece is dead,
    a woman is dead,
    a boy is dead,
    because I see me and you
    want to play with bodies
    words cut, too,
    and orchestras melt
    into ruined theaters

> while tuxedo-clad clowns
> clap their hands.

The species wearing a fashionable necktie.
> Maybe the Beatles walked
> across this valley
> but Doc, I have to say,
> I remember your face
> and the wife who left you
> because you went mad,
> and found that my wife
> is just as willing to die
> for a greater cause,
> I mean,
> an experiment.

# VINCENZO BILOF

# Nerve Endings

Your honor, brain patterns coalesce,
collide,

Lorraine,
she wanted to save me

Inept
to speak before you

Flesh
withers in the jury box

Skulls
peeling while I sleep

Magistrate
clad in nowhere today

Abyss
within the folds of your robe

("But they won't put me on trial will they, the laws of
experimentation
                    dictate you know, dictate, expose
                    the brain patterns
                    observe waves")

Whispers
cut through gravity

# THE HORROR SHOW

White
tables and room, doctors and men

Severance
mind stem electrons conjugated

Medicate
the race of man for dollars

Immortality
here's what we can buy


Spectral
bicycles upon the stars

Fantasy
the quest for Christ's eyes

("She was the one or you were the one I am the vehicle
    of your failure
    your pride
    your greed
    encapsulate these patterns
    cap the bottle").

# CHAPTER TWELVE

## Visitations Again

# Love Song for the Prisoner

Cracks along the glass stairwell
you could have broken me
a thousand times broken
me

      What should I say now?
      Your lords remove my presence
      replace the carpet
      among the missing.

            Is there something I should forgive?
            Ascension unto me,
            these gossamer fingertips
            would still trace the holes beneath
            your eyes.

Slip into something more comfortable
who can say you were here
upon this field of flame
or this oil-stained heaven

      Afterthoughts murmured the rapture
      a spine of teeth
      how breakfast tastes soggy, cold
      a corpse without a face

This time was not mine
Daddy smiled and vanished
suddenly elapsed
youth surrendered to tragedy

# VINCENZO BILOF

        You're not worth the hour to haunt
        the emotion and the pain
        all life, poured into a skull
        heart held captive in a picture frame

Love. The ultimate death before death
is a moment of pause
waves cresting the tidal pull in slow-motion
invading shorelines where strangers live forever

                Count to twelve with me
                I can hold my breath
now

                captured, puzzle-pieces
                when young men held
my hand

                and felt like dukes

Ask me if I want it all back
or a prophet will be murdered
or a bird will sing
stars drift into light and orgasmic
unity of thought, mortality

        You know who I am
        no piano will play for me
        no out-of-tune harpsichord
        or a blind man crying behind
        movable walls

The comedy of regret
the horror of the past
watch this smirk fade
I stood before the dead
every day
do you want to know if I'm mad

I say unto you

# THE HORROR SHOW

the gods have all drowned
do you want to know if I'm mad.

        The stairwell again
        life is forever
        it dies and it dies
        do you want.

**VINCENZO BILOF**

## We Can Feel Sad Now

    seas of misfortune incomplete travesty

listening for thunder
                archangels sliding swords into their bellies


the sewage of chuckling burns
an asylum where the water is waist-high

remora glow of midnight


no legs just a head maybe a pair of hands
listening for thunder
drained           the choke
                      of yield
                                  dismembered
from the neck down
son of a man

touch me again for we are not here today
softly the smoke cools
                    inside there is a mind
                    or the ants are singing to their queen

                        drift

                                          ing
(thunder has a name)

## Mrs. Every

Ha ha ha
You see these black gloves
this is what I remember

from us

Sigh.

> (I forgot to close your ears
> when he screamed
> against the train
> the torment
> the storm
> his rage
> the prophecy of you)

I wanted you to be lovely, a noir romance
only gray is the color of fathoms

I do. I do. I do.

Danny was such a good boy
      (Grandson, I remember,
      the impossible
      Grandson)
you were his father in those last moments
just don't let the blade

oh.

misspeak. theaters blackened by rain

# VINCENZO BILOF

every lover wants their story
tablets delivered from a mountaintop

etched. you and I. elevators from the ocean
into the sky where ravens are blue

*noir cycled into decades*

on your desk or on the kitchen table maybe on the couch maybe
on the floor
disappear from me. enslaved by white spaces
the ambivalence

suffering. sleeping.
you slay me with your eyes again and again

THE HORROR SHOW

# If Only We Could Die Again

The sound of years burning
    guilt
        thunderstorms  carnivals in the mud

freak show can remove breasts and beat a dead horse

stay in the car and watch

      you never deserved so much as a hug

your father, what a man
trampled                 but what a fucking metaphor
that is

why don't you write poems about candles and ravens and ghosts and blood
maybe zombies or vampires or werewolves or goblins or nightmares

what is        I don't know this son

ask me when death
is supposed to feel empty
          remorse has fattened my eyes
          no

heart
    to break      this son

tents collapse in bronze glory bleeding dirt
    some dust in a gremlin's beard
    a dwarf who forgot he was alive

# VINCENZO BILOF

stop feeding the corpses
        these dead men run the show

words                stay
                        in the car

my commands                        not your mother like you like
                      versions twisted
stories on bricks
                      strippers without legs

where is the madness in thunder
        afraid of real

sleep

you waste hats and gloves          shelters cobwebbed
        hours of dark

"it's a boy," they all said

but I wept and told them to take you away
        I haven't slept

a Chinese woman with a penis stuck in her armpit

        she was like a mother to you
which

smiling sideways            necks upside-down
everything blinks twice while rolling backward on a rubber ball

you chose all the colors
whoever said I was dead

lied.

# THE HORROR SHOW

## Operant Conditioning

Cracking through novels and burning the shelves
along pathways which conclude elsewhere

You think murder is personal son,
*a grin from ear to ear now, you're smiling
wherever you think you might be*

Maybe I did you favor only I don't
see it that way. Dad is a puppet
*Deus ex machina* like a fireball
in the mouth

beg for these galaxies the expansion
of sin, monsters perched upon the satellites
touch each key softly, son, words explode

w     h     a     t     a     p     o     l
      o     g     y

?
a red hand emerges
out of screens,

grasping my face
pulling, ripping from reality
emotion, so now you know an artist
from a forgery, all bundled up in
Starbucks for conformity

standing ovations are worth souls
you're the one I killed for

# VINCENZO BILOF

aren't you . . .
proud of your father?

# CHAPTER THIRTEEN

## Upon an Ivory Coast

# The Students
## (When I Can See Again)

All the shoelaces are tied today.
    Skin-shaded heels.
    Women behind glass.
    Mouths unmoving, unmovable.
    Centuries-gripped notepads.
    Electric or otherwise.
    Something hums the same.

Opinions and theories become laws
because purple is green where blue is red
although, that's because the aliens
called in to work today
sick behind machines.

Binary code speeches.
    (through speakers)
    Warned not to peer over the curtain.
    Smooth fingers trace life-scans, rainbow language.
    Doors closing in ice-cubed hallways.

Water-sucking lips make
the sound of frogs in a desert
where there is no sun.
Look at them: strangers who don't
recognize themselves.
Why aren't they afraid?
Why aren't they shaking?
Don't they know they aren't real?
Maybe they've come to bury Ceasar.
I mean, it's the only thing I can think of.

# VINCENZO BILOF

## Erasure

        They will question my methods

What does Colonel Kurtz think?
Allow me to introduce the mind on two planes
      Insanity by design

For the low-low price
flooded tree-branch pathways
Lightning flashes in a snowstorm
A state of Union:
                "Dear Gentlemen (rehearse the
                enterprise)
                pardon the icebreaker
                one day you'll have to stop living
                my tomb... an imaginary plane,
                androids playing with blocks,
                here is"
MELTED, THE COGNITION!

Electronic spinal fusion to memory. The solution:

dismay.

Let the rebels ring the bells in the name of madness!
To save mankind it must be destroyed
watch this virus spin between my fingers
        Trust in me we cannot fail in this
      The flesh sacrifice to save the soul of the mind
           Burning money into bones
              This will be the messiah
           Pure chaos to create order

# THE HORROR SHOW

We can see ourselves out of balance
\*\*\*

"I don't feel comfortable"

"I had high expectations. But then again, you knew."

"I'll always be a professional" (and there you have it,
a precious way of life in jeopardy but there
will be salvation at all costs)

"Millions of dollars are lost. This is where you explain why it was"
(clears throat)
"excuse me, wasn't a total waste."

"You shouldn't think of it as failure. A man was insane and for a brief
period he was not. I've looked over the research and I've spent a good
period of my life just . . . look,
my family has . . . sacrificed . . . and I just think . . . "

"There are some dead people who have their own definition" (the
colonel looks askance, looking at the light bulb hanging over the desk
as if
a fly has found a home there)

"You wanted a cure, something we can use. I'm not Christ though we
seem to (stop right there before you say "look for his guise withering in
the labs where immortality hides")"

"That's enough. Can insanity be cured?"

"The human mind has not gone digital. We operate on that premise
and devise a . . . a . . .
software update . . . upload it to . . . "

"If the mind can be cured it can be modified, transformed, used,
applied. We need warriors of logic. No more murders on my
bases, no more civilians killed or trials . . . "

"But this, I mean, the mind cannot be just a weapon there are thoughts and things we cannot see, miracles and wonders behind the electricity, the network (swallow because you've heard this before mumbled in poetic verse)"

"Liabilities. I'm looking at liabilities. Another dead girl. Butchered, not even dead."

"Maybe cure the human race of itself. Murder was the byproduct, and she volunteered for death. She fell in love and that's the end of that. We know where loves takes us. Places . . ."

(Is this a conversation about horror or love? Money or responsibility? Someone's job will be killed and the colonel is about to interject, tell you
you're wrong, tell you
that love is not worth the money invested)

(Let the conversation become one about fear, let's see if we can talk about philosophy)

"Doctor, I'm afraid you don't know what we've wasted, here."

"I'm not finished with him. Give me more time. His mind is beautiful, a work of art."

(The colonel laughed and snorted, the word "art" mumbled through his veil, because he'll never understand, never understand)

There is a meta-poem, verse coagulated,
there is a mind connected by wires
data synthetic, consciousness plugged
the future of code

"Results are necessary. We need a cure for this mind, or you'll have blood"
(on your hands, say it, on your hands.)

# THE HORROR SHOW

<pre>
                         ***
I'm afraid I don't know how to apologize.
Remember when we met?              This is where
memory speaks.
Your name was Sister Detroit.      You were a saint before
I had you killed.
A book of poetry on your lap.
I wasn't hungry for soup.

What have you today? What brought you
to this moment? You were the perfect
blood sacrifice. Innocent, (quick to laugh)
you were doomed. I knew.           I can't
remember the book of poems you were
                                       reading. I think
it might be important
                                   a symbol or an
artifact; you should be buried
           now, if only there was enough left to
                                              inter.
It was never about the money.
Hymns from an occult novel
paperback trash where the men
love for the sake of love.         Why weren't you reading
something as simple
            as that?
A part of me is scattered among
the pieces. An ideal. The men
will mourn you but after tomorrow
you will cease.                    I remember a story
about you. A man who
                                       broke into your
apartment to find it bare,
                                       (a television not
even worth stealing
                                       a couch not
even worth pissing on)
                                       and smelling
</pre>

# VINCENZO BILOF

like dying cats;

                                    and they looked

at you and took pity

                                    because you

smiled and offered them

                everything, not even rape

                                    it was like

killing something that

                                    wasn't even

  there;

                                    the storyteller

said he couldn't compare

                                  the moment to

killing a child

                                  because of

where he lived, in the fire

                                   of sorrow, in

circles where

                                  streets don't

have light and the houses

                                  have holes in

them.

\*\*\*

The scientific method--
behold, the masterpiece!
One slice of mind here
and it no longer matters, does it?
This monster breathes
for the sake of the real!

I shall call it SANE because it
knows what it is.
Everyone gets their money's worth

a beast made of porn
a sentence fragment
capital letters and a dead child
two lovers

# THE HORROR SHOW

They don't know!
This is me, my ultimate;
a prophet with a name older
than textbooks;
pictograms and gods choking

>dancing now, dancing
>"holy mountains burning bright
>let this lover take a bite
>he's the one who knows your soul
>he drinks your blood from a bowl
>the perfect man made of dreams
>limbs attached with a thousand seams
>we shared the madness of the years
>I wrote it down while he shed tears
>nightmare man, nightmare man
>kills whatever a nightmare can."

Can't you see we're all the same?
blood and bone and things
dripping between spaces

an ocean of life on my hands
everything so pretty
red in water can become pink

>He clenches his fists
>he rises to his feet
>heroes and martyrs
>video melodrama
>melted into a microchip
>a cure for insanity
>a cure of mortality
>a cure for the human race
>they'll thank me once they're
>all

# VINCENZO BILOF

Dead. If only he knew my eyes
if only his hands
weren't soaked in marrow
Lorraine was a waste
Lorraine I spit on your

I spit on your

*innocence is insanity*
the murder is the world
the murder is the world
and everything can be hot or cold
even these hands.

# THE HORROR SHOW

## Like a Scene from a Movie that Might Not Be Good Anymore

Patchwork dead people look funny
when they're standing over you.
In the last Star Wars movie, you know
the third one, or the sixth one,
dead people smiled when someone's world
ended, and people celebrated death.
Little beasties jumping around a fire
with robots and a couple tall humans,
and maybe there was a black guy,
I can't remember.

My feet smell, and as a rule
of thumb,
I don't have to get used to
hallucinating. The mystery
of me is fun, but now
I feel like a meat-on-meat sandwich
with pus instead of mustard
and it's crowded at this party,
so maybe I should wave
and wait for them to talk.

Funny, I don't remember Danny
being so tall.

**VINCENZO BILOF**

# If Ulysses Wore His Sunglasses

Lorraine: You were never supposed to be cured.

Connie: How many of us want to hold your hand?

Danny: Mrs. Turnbuckle thought it would be great if you could come in one day and talk about writing and poetry. We're about to do some poetry in class and she said if we had a *real* poet in the room it would be a great experience.

Mom: I'll turn the music down but only for a moment. Listen to the way Kenny G goes to town. Cute little baby. How you love Kenny G. You're going to be a musician someday just like him. Louder?

Lorraine: My father was wearing silk underwear when he died. I remember hearing my mom say that. He wanted to come home and make love to my mom.

A Pretty Girl: You're still cute, even with blood on your face. I remember saying that. You could get the best coke man, dig it. Good shit. You only live once, anyway.

Danny: I don't know any of these people. Mom acts strange sometimes. She told me once she wanted to write poems but decided she would become an adult instead. You were in the room when she said it and your nose started bleeding. I didn't say anything.

An Old Man with Fleas Dancing in His Beard: Ugh. Fucking cold. Need a good fire for these bones. Come on over here, boy. Least I could do. You won't find too many people sharing fires out here. Got a soft spot for you. I remember saying that to you but I didn't know you could see the broken beer bottle. Man, I thought I had you. Thought you would bleed, for sure.

A Rat: Lemons are my favorite thing to eat.

## The Sex of the Ocean

Puzzle pieces taste the same
    *in nomine scientiae*

          Pause the transgression
          Sweat and desperation
          a maze of stairwells
    Escher-painted bodies gliding

gears churn where the storm haunts a boy
poetry born from fear behind windows

          Conductors full of heat
            the grind of teeth
              crows flying headlong into lava

(tombstone in a barrel full of apples
names written in cursive
with a flourish, all men are created————hair matted to brain)

mushrooms blossom in winter
lightning slits, the lingerie of clouds
how many promises at this feast

    it's all syrup
    this is how we swim in people

the core of a spine
all the good doctors have passed this way to a tower
doves whispering epic verse in the vein of Geraldo

# VINCENZO BILOF

      soul-encrusted fingernails
      weeds gasping for air (veins, veins and thunderclouds)
      *in nomine scientiae*

Flip to page seven hundred and eight my beating meat slabs

here's a woman who found herself in an oven
      she said, "execute me again with your eyes"

all I've known
are the policies of Saturn

at the top of the stairs is a box
Pandora speaks from the cellar
      "touch me here, and I'll never forgive you"

      the feast is delightful and you're welcome
rock and roll stars of our generation
the phallic monsters

monitors display the gore of dead girls
the pleasure of pain

      you can do whatever you want to them
*in nomine scientiae*
                                       Latin gargoyles scratch
   the buttocks

toys on the lawn processed into teeth
I can taste you forever and paint
           faces in words, a mother and a son
           they're dead
           a pretty girl like a bird
           spaghetti-stains you can't get out of your clothes
    or hair

*in nomine scientiae*

# THE HORROR SHOW

let them walk in an see us that's part of the thrill
Pandora you whelp
    you bitch you you you
    open the box to let the machine breathe again
    give me back my fingers
    I can taste my madness

nothing else smells like an orgasm underwater
breathe deeply and shudder
hollow, all
    of these heads
    liquid time smells like pennies.

# IN THE NAME OF SCIENCE

Spider Exorcist

Voices trickle into
the hollow
throat

chemical words
splattered onto the wall

the specimen retches     cobwebs     all silk nothings
Martian prayers
spilled words          collect     in veins

Doctor Humphrey
faces captured here,

in his blood,
this is where art is born
in tornado-mouths

(a door opens
      fucking masks again
      beware the infected
      we are in you
      we are here
      everywhere
                  inside
      warm graves
      and dusty
      worms)

upon which altar     does the     predictable

# THE HORROR SHOW

                            symbolic funeral-
                            scented

candle wither

what, children

have we learned today?

                                            "The Horror . . ."

Doctor lies face down    hole in the back——how? Theories;
choked bigger
than killer not sure. Attacker

get background——what do we know? Experiment. Doctor's
results questioned.

Someone went mad,
they say. There was a poet involved.

We invested money in this. A cure for insanity.
Looking through doctor's notes.
He believed it. Faith in madness. This was him. An impetus or
definition. When did catharsis . . . ? Thought he was designing a
monster worth dreading. Reverse the
flow of nightmare and create a man who lives in . . . two worlds . . .
the subconscious and . . .

aren't we all there now? Between faith and nothing.
                            blood scrawled,
something I can think.
WAS I INSANE

No reason to preserve body. His mind is all we need. Removal

imminent. I've decided.
Doctor in a pool he made, his own, his fault or mine.

White floor carpeted in red. Or an ocean designed by a storm.
Thinking today. No more begging for more money from the colonel.
In the jungle

there is darkness and in the darkness

      there is the mind and the savage and the emotion.
Twisted into people.

Musings aloud. Ha. What if I said
these things.

Sentences of something. Comes around to me where it started.
Murder and
entrails. Messages and dreams. Part of the job, of course. Would the doctor know this mind?

Have a feeling if we cure insanity
we all die like the doctor.

I can be the leader of the revolution or a martyr I would die first
is that peace when eyes close or the
afterimages linger
a wife a child, maybe the mother, a girl, a doctor, victims
of sorcery.

Journals are for men who don't know when to surrender to the organism
the pulsing organism pumps,
sewers running
undercarriage of the soul
penises and vaginas suspended in motion
whoever can burn the money of all
      whoever can look for brains

tells them all in headlines
a species among us

                    And I could tell you all about madness

but

                    then I might be telling the truth
                    those aren't in my orders
                    the ones I give, the ones I share
                    no matter how many have to live
                    riding the creaky hamster wheel

      transcripts


HIS FIRST NIGHTMARE WAS ABOUT A STORM. HE WAS A CHILD AND THEN A TEENAGER AND THEN A MAN. HE WAS AFRAID AND WE KNOW THE STORM CANNOT END. IT CANNOT BE OVERCOME. THE STORM PERSISTS.

# THE HORROR SHOW

## Dear Danny,

*You're a young man, now. Several years ago, I watched you emerge into the world. As my fingers hammer away at the keyboard, that was one year ago today.*

*This is a moment where I must be honest with you, and myself. I don't know what kind of man you will know; my future self is a stranger who may or may not be me. While I've managed to eke out a comfortable living as a poet in a world that may only have room enough for one living poet, I cannot assume you will enjoy my verse or my words, which are two different things, of course.*

*I have already written this message several times, but I have now entered the phase where I must be honest with the*

*computer screen so that I can, at last, be honest with you.*

*Your mother is not aware that I'm a narcissist. I want a world free of distraction where I might know myself through*

*words, for I fail to make sense of my own affliction. I can only hope that science, with all of its miracles, can cure the narcolepsy. I hope you understand; I suffer from a mild form of amnesia that, some doctors theorize, may become worse.*

*I wanted to be a good man for you. I hope, by the time you read this, that you still enjoy the great American past time*

*we call baseball. Your grandfather was cannibalized by a storm, and since then, I've been obsessed with loud music and memories that may or may not be my own.*

*Doctor Humphrey has agreed to help me. In a strange way, I feel like it's a blood oath; if he can't cure me, then I must be removed to a place where I can't hurt anybody. The sight of blood makes me queasy; I hope I've done nothing to hurt you.*

*Your grandmother is a narcissist, too. In love with her damn operas, as if you didn't know already. I wanted her to*

*send me away a long time ago because I was afraid of myself. But all my teachers thought I was a nice kid, and nobody complained. At least, I never found out about it. I thought I was a boring kid who liked video games, fireflies, and baseball.*

*Love is a foreign concept to me. I didn't know what the hell it was, really. I mean, sex is fun, as you'll find out (or maybe you have already? what kind of father have I been to you? what kind of devil have I cursed you with?). Love, on the other hand, is a majestic, chaotic force that refuses to be understood by even the most learned philosophers. Gravity, life, afterlife, and love; concepts and questions that haunt our minds, but we're all experts in these subjects.*

*Danny, you have taught me what it is.*

*Your mother is better poet than I, and she risked her*

idea of art and tragedy to give me a chance, because we both wanted to find love. We wanted to find you, but we didn't know it.

There is no judgment in your eyes; only acceptance. Pure, uncorrupted joy that I am in your presence. Laughter filled with the desire to laugh more, because there is always time enough for laughter, and nothing else. Your reality is defined only by the very pleasure of being alive, even while you have no idea what being "alive" means. Well, shit, that's a whole 'nother barrel o' monkeys, innit?

Love is possible. There aren't enough words nor is there a language that can explain what it is or how it feels. There are

many poets who believe they can explain to all of us, and several talk show hosts who seem to have the answer, but there is something that only a parent can know, but cannot describe. I want the courage to be able to finish this, to give it to you, because I have been weakened and devastated by this truth. It's wonderful to know there are things I cannot know but can feel. A reality beyond reality. Another plane between the subconscious, the physical mind, and a fleshy thing we call the body. I want the courage to finish this, to keep going, but I am only explaining my thought to my one, true wife, which dutifully listens but offers nothing which may serve as a satisfactory answer. It stares at me, and behind its glare there is power. Danny, I hope you will hear me. I hope you will know me. I hope I will finish this before my soul shrivels and it's too late to find what this all means to me. Before I forget.

# EPILOGUE
# (Voices Underwater)

## Puzzle Pieces

### THE HORROR SHOW

# "Let's See What's on the Two O'Clock News"

Time to ride the spiral.

Explain what narcolepsy is, explain the nightmares, explain my hopelessness and despair, "you're always so nice to me, a smile and a wink."

Streaks of light and a couch that squeaks, thin fabric procured from a lawn on garbage day.
I'm okay really, I'm okay they won't tell you that

………………………they. Let's talk about they:

White-collared gods who trade bullets for children,
you're afraid of a murderer you don't know,
accept the killers who rule
behind the stockings of tired mistresses.

Here is where a picture of your boyfriend should have been.
Don't be afraid if I share,
a thought about his teeth raking across your flesh,
your eyelashes becoming desperate butterflies.

I've heard your tragedy before:

If something happens to me you
lose the sounding board
who sits with ham and eggs and nods

his head, chewing carefully.

They say words in black,

# VINCENZO BILOF

oil spilling through mouths;
liars and jesters within the court of a skeleton king,
here I thought we had something in common.

If you lose me you can't tell anyone else
about the things you've lost and the things you've given up
because every man
just wants to eat you alive.

# THE HORROR SHOW

## "It's Already Quarter to Three?"

. . . out this dead urban landscape.
There is an angry longing for the unkept promises,
little whispers whirling in the shadows of doorways—
winking in and out of a wintry past that has cracked
the wind along the stone
—erosion a blade—
the whispers like wind-song rumors.

My place is right this way. Don't be a stranger.
Let's be courteous now, this is a tomb, and here we respect the
forever silenced.

Not quite the 8$^{th}$ circle with you as my guide.
    (my light, my love, my shining star
    my need, my fury, my everlasting need)
Repeat after me:

A diatribe! A diatribe!
wondering how your flesh might taste,
salty the smell of grease and ash
forever staining the nape of your neck
so young, so lovingly imperfect

A total ruin;
a train crashing through a glacier,

an engine powered by the cackling of eighty five eighty-five-year-old
clowns.

We belong here.
WE SHOULD BE FLOCKING with the dirt and the rocks

between our toes in the ruins of an ancient, empty city
only I am here
I am here with you
only I am here
here with you,

the ghost continued.

# THE HORROR SHOW

## The Return of the Prisoner

The cockroach king sits upon his throne of dust,
a kingdom reserved

> (and you wanted, this, a walk through ages of loneliness
> and the disease of thought, the corruption
> of emotion,
> the wailing of a maimed identity)

for bed sheets and silences. Legions uncontested,
spindly legs, invincible creatures
chattering madly for Kafka's metaphor.

This is where I live, upon the lap
of malaise where prophets have laid their
heads down to die quietly,
cockroaches marching through their nostrils,
traversing the corridors where the eyes should be,
a mead hall where brain is served upon
trembling plates.

Pity the worms who've lost the war for the dead.
This is where I live, not in Hell;
a darker hole between torment and ecstasy,
a hermitage or a kingdom.

I am the unwanted guest in the realm
of inevitable,
the cockroach king who waves goodbye
to sunsets and carefully-planned murders.

# Sale for the Century

Riding a bike down a broad street the cars pass him by and a plastic
bag dangles from his handlebars

(is that what he envisioned, I wonder, is that what he would have
wanted as a young boy, I wonder.)

Fantasies for a woman who doesn't exist.
Maybe black and white pictures
burn in tin cans
without permission,
just like other lies.

(Not safe to wonder
aloud, maybe buy a lonely paperback, avoid the darting and
drifting eyes of the perverts, pretend to

admire the low prices; I should seem pleased and thankful that
the boys staring at my ass want to put groceries
into my cart.

Maybe you and I with your dead-poet eyes
could walk through

the bright aisles with your shirt halfway
unbuttoned; you could have been a Bohemian

but instead you became an overnight narcoleptic. A wanted man

lost in thought but not in the consciousness of fear that pervades
over the television sets brightly illuminating the living rooms of
dying mothers.

# THE HORROR SHOW

A celebrity now,
an experiment in diner-breakfast conversation.
What drove you mad? What broke your mind and your heart all at once? Was it the money
that kept pouring in? Maybe everything wasn't meant for you; a man out of time and place,

dead centuries ago—a warrior poet with the name of your fair maiden on your cold, pale lips, a vision of her flowing hair forever freezing your eyes;

they threw you into a mass-grave ,the battle over and done.
You sacrificed

daytime hours sitting on a bench watching your son play ball in his

expensive sneakers————————————you mentioned it in a poem;

you invested in the future of investing in his future; tear it all down with your hands and your wife's final gasp for air you

should be locked up, but you belong
between nowhere and the machinations of a doctor as mad as you wonder what will happen when I call the number on the screen

will it save

your or someone else's life?
What is there to save in you?)

A man dejectedly sits on the sidewalk with his head in his hands.
Give him a coin or two and say
hello to pass the time,
fuck his brains out and tell him
you've had a good time;
hark! the angels sing and we've got unlimited time to talk on

# VINCENZO BILOF

our phones but that time is not free, you pay for time
everything on sale
the savings are incredible. These are the things
you'll never remember
because you weren't awake.

# The Sound of an Epilogue in an Empty Theater

A committed crime smells like someone else's homemade remedy
Some convergence upon an age-old enemy
Glimmer in the dreams of a dead Aristophanes
A dedicated sports fan who shouts "Oh my God you gotta be kidding me"

Call it eight-point-five million for a dedicated cause not worth mentioning
An old man turns on his TV to see the murder of John F. Kennedy
All these futures laugh from ahead of me
Now I'll send you to an over-crowded and dark cemetery

I know a girl who has an umbrella of blond hair over a slender neckline
Tall like she's from a madman's vision of nineteen eighty-nine
Tight red leather jacket that will always keep its glossy cheap shine
Now she's dead and nobody knows I enjoyed the crime

Draw this on a bathroom wall above a drunk or dead legendary musician
Life will always feel like you're breathing through a cellophane imitation
That which you clamor for is not worth any man's quiet desperation
Or the memory of you lying prostrate for a final visitation Like a rock star you need to be shot down in flames
As if you never belonged because everybody's the same
A smile worth a hundred of your lifetimes is no definition of the mundane

The reason why we'll endure 8.5 million years of pain

# VINCENZO BILOF

What concept is worth your visionary consideration A childhood fetish of success without moderation
Consider identity confusion the height of your imagination
Lay down your arms and rest with the congregation Lay down your arms and rest
With the congregation

# THE HORROR SHOW

# Confessions from the Street Generation, In the Year 2001 in the Month of April

The killers in the streets think about you
Dream about blue and red lights,
Post-mortem lights and the frosted tile
A place where Quiet rests.

The killers in the streets dance with
Madness and caress
the self-stylized impersonal interview.
I might've seen dead people
And we've all seen dead pigs.

    What other love and devotion to you need than
    the suffering of the impoverished?
    Grab a fistful of ash
    Sprinkle ghosts onto the stone steps
                         of tired churches where
we die more than once
    in beds cleaned with sweat instead of soap.

a profound dedication to suffering.
And you talk about economies of scale

    Lady Liberty that's who,
    up her skirts the birth of that war
    war full of terror, souls full of lead,
    all at the mercy of dreamers
    numbers from their owners.
    And you call me crazy? To be crazy
    is to inherit the possibilities of an
    unreachable future and die for them.

# VINCENZO BILOF

Look for a prophet in the alleys where children are born
Word on the street was written in his book
While fathers burn their dreams in dumpsters.

Yeah, maybe he lived here in the brick
for a few hundred years.

# About The Author

Vincenzo Bilof is an engineer who works at the Packard Plant in Detroit, Michigan. This is his first novel. Forthcoming titles include: *Gregorian Chants Sung Backward By the Japanese National Choir*, and *The Idiot's Guide to Noir Fiction*. Both will be published in 2015 from Black Swan Press.

## All Art is Junk by R. A. Harris

Lana Rivers, a girl with paintbrush hair, is missing and it's up to Lancelot, her cyborg knight, and his bionic conjoined twin, Cilia, to find her before her evil father, a disrespected artist turned mad-scientist, performs a terrible experiment on her.

## Cherub by David C. Hayes

Cherub wasn't like the other boys—too slow, too rough—but he didn't deserve what that hospital did to him, and now he will make them pay.

## Skinners by Adam Millard

Los Angeles, the City of Angels. At least, that's what the brochure says. What it fails to mention is the earthquakes. Oh, and the flesh-eating creatures lying dormant beneath the concrete, waiting for the chance to surface once again. Their wait is over . . .

## The After-Life Story of Pork Knuckles Malone by MP Johnson

What's a farm boy to do when his pet pig becomes an evil, decaying hunk of ham with slime-spewing psychic powers?

## A Lightbulb's Lament by Grant Wamack

A gentleman with a lightbulb for head wakes up in a world full of darkness, hooks up with a beautiful ex-prostitute, and an old man who can heal people; he travels down south to find the mysterious Creator.

## The Horror Show by Vincenzo Bilof

A poetry novel—a narcoleptic, amnesiac Nobel Prize-winning poet becomes the subject of an experiment to cure madness.

## Beyond by Jordan Krall

From Jerusalem to Mars, psychiatry and the unraveling of the universe

## Gravity Comics Massacre
## by Vincenzo Bilof

An absolutely shitty novella involving comic books, aliens, a serial killer, teenagers in an abandoned town, horror-trope dream sequences, and an ending you're going to hate.

## Glue by Scott Lange

Sticky bowels and sticky situations.

## Ascent by Matthew Bialer

Is the 8 foot tall creature haunting a small town in Iowa in the fall of the year 1903 the product of a hoax and collective imagination or was it one of the first documented paranormal event in America? This epic poem grapples with these questions.

## Fecal Terror by David Bernstein

A killer turd is on the loose!

## The Fairy Princess of Trains
## by Christopher Boyle

Danny's mediocre life turns upside-down when his couch starts whispering to him. Then he's charged with a supernatural mission: Rescue the Fairy Princess of Trains.

## Terence, Mephisto & Viscera Eyes
## by Chris Kelso

9 new science fiction stories from Chris Kelso

## How to Succesfully Kidnap Strangers by Max Booth III

Do not respond to bad reviews. If you must respond to bad reviews, please do not kidnap the reviewer.

# Bizarro Bizarro: An Anthology

The finest bizarro short stories from 2013.

# Necrosaurus Rex by Nicolas Day

Necrosaurus Rex tells the tale of Martin, a simple janitor, who takes an unfortunate trip through time, becomes a violent mutant, and the father of us all. There's 14 billion years crushed inside these pages, and most of them are pretty nasty.

# Day of the Milkman by S. T. Cartledge

In a world dominated by the milk industry, only one milkman survives after a terrible storm sinks all the ships and throws the Great White Sea out of balance.

# Moosejaw Frontier by Chris Kelso

An unapologetic disaster of metafiction

# Notes from the Guts of a Hippo by Grant Wamack

A rugged journalist travels to Brazil in search of a missing hippo researcher and the notes left behind lead to something earth shatteringly revelatory.

# Industrial Carpet Drag by Bruce Taylor

Chemicals make you do great things!

# ADHD Vampire by Matthew Vaughn

He came, he conquered, he was distracted a lot

www.ingramcontent.com/pod-product-compliance
Lightning Source LLC
Chambersburg PA
CBHW061427040426
42450CB00007B/933